Inlander Histories

Volume 1

EDITED BY TED S. McGREGOR JR.

INLAND NORTHWEST HISTORY, SPOKANE HISTORY, NORTH IDAHO HISTORY

ON THE COVER:
"SALMON CHIEF" SCULPTURE BY VIRGIL MARCHAND
AT THE LOWER FALLS OF THE SPOKANE RIVER IN HUNTINGTON PARK
INLANDER MAY 2014 PHOTO BY YOUNG KWAK / COVER DESIGN BY CHRIS BOVEY

INLANDER BOOKS
1227 W. SUMMIT PARKWAY
SPOKANE, WASHINGTON 99201
INLANDER.COM/BOOKS

ISBN-13: 978-0692313367 / ISBN-10: 0692313362

INLANDER *Histories*

Timeless Tales of Spokane and the Inland Northwest, Volume 1

inlanderbooks

SPOKANE, WASHINGTON
INLANDER.COM/BOOKS

TABLE OF CONTENTS

WELCOME TO INLANDER HISTORIES

Since the very start of the *Inlander* back in 1993, I knew I wanted to make local history a part of the mix of stories we'd present in our pages. People connect with a place by the stories they tell. Native Americans of the Plateau tribes did; they have a vibrant tradition of stories unique to this part of the continent that helped them explain their world. And since this place was settled by newcomers, Spokane and the Inland Northwest have generated a lot of amazing stories, too — stories that explain how we got here and where we're heading. Here in *Inlander Histories*, we've collected some of the best stories we've published.

Every one has its own backstory. Maybe it was something I lived through as a kid, like the eruption of Mt. St. Helens. Often the ideas were brought to me by local historians like Jack Nisbet. No matter how we came up with the idea, the writers would throw themselves at the project and the results would light up the pages of our newspaper. It's been a privilege for me to work with such great writers, along with our team here at the *Inlander*, and to be able to share these stories over the years.

But 21 years into the life of the *Inlander*, I started thinking about our archive of historical articles (many of which have been out of print for more than a decade) and how I didn't want them to be forgotten. These stories deserve a longer shelf-life. So here it is, *Inlander Histories*.

You'll notice the random nature of this collection. Over the years, we've documented everything from the song "White Christmas" to a mysterious gravestone in Moscow, Idaho, to my own grandfather, Joe Peirone. I hope it's kind of like our newspaper, where we aim to surprise you but also offer something for everyone. And in case you're wondering, yes, we did name this "Volume 1" for a reason. We've still got more *Inlander Histories* where these came from.

I hope you enjoy these stories as much as I have.

Ted S. McGregor Jr.
Inlander founder and publisher
October 23, 2014

A trilobite fossil in red shale found in Spokane County.

LINDA McCOLLUM PHOTO

Signs of Life, Spokane County

BY JACK NISBET

First published in the *Inlander* on February 10, 2005

Anyone who looks at rocks in the Columbia Basin south of the Spokane River sees mostly basalt — volcanic magma cooled into a delightful variety of layers, flutes and swirls. Students hear stories of magma bubbling up from cracks in the Snake River country to flow elastically north and blanket the entire region; of layers thousands of feet thick; of Lake Missoula floods crashing down from the northeast to carve the world we see now around Spokane and in the Cheney-Palouse scablands. Teachers place the basalt flows in the Miocene Period, from 17 million to 7 million years before the present. They crack open cakes of clay that built up between eruptive incidents and show off fossil imprints of leaves and needles from familiar forest trees as proof that a long time ago this was a wet, warm place.

But what lies beneath all those layers of basalt? Steptoes of very old rock in the Palouse hint at limitless possibilities. In the early part of the 20th century, oil wildcatters wondered if black gold might be one of them, and drilled test holes throughout the Columbia Basin. Some years ago, Department of Natural Resources geologist Bob Derkey ran across a 1919 drill log from lower Latah Creek that had broken through the basalt and recorded "shells, fossils" in the middle of the usual notations of clays and gravel. The usual Latah clays yield fossil plants from fresh water environments of the Miocene Period; "shells" hinted at the remains of animals from an ancient saltwater sea, and at dates far earlier than that.

❖ ❖ ❖

On a spring afternoon in April 2002, Derkey and DNR colleague Mike Hamilton decided to investigate a wrinkle in the landscape near Clear Lake, just off Interstate 90 in western Spokane County. Derkey, in the midst of reworking the geologic map of the county, was interested an outcrop of old limestone in the vicinity, but upon their arrival both geologists were struck by a scattering of peculiar red shale visible along the roadside and around some telephone poles. Hamilton, who grew up in the Midwest and was used to associating such shale with fossils, sat down among the red chunks and began to whack at their laminations with his rock hammer. It wasn't long before he found himself staring at the tail of a trilobite, one of the most ancient and revealing fossil types. Both geologists knew of trilobite sites to the north, but there were no records of such ancient fossils within dozens of miles of Spokane County.

Hamilton and Derkey took samples of the mudstone back to Eastern Washington University and showed them to Linda McCollum in the geology department. McCollum happens to specialize in trilobites, and for years has taken thousand-mile field trips to southern Nevada to study a range of trilobites in very old formations of Great Basin bedrock. She is especially interested in a fossil called *Glossopleura*—- a relatively large, distinctive and common trilobite whose life span can be used to determine the boundary between epochs in different strata of Great Basin rocks. When McCollum recognized a *Glossopleura* trilobite peering at her, from a rock collected just a few miles from her classroom in Cheney, it was clear proof that the reddish shale had been formed in a marine environment during what geologists the Middle Cambrian Period, more than 500 million years ago.

The geologists had to find out exactly where this red shale came from. The rise where they found the scattered chunks was part of a Fairchild Air Force Base recreational site at Clear Lake, so McCollum and her husband Mike applied for a permit to make further investigations. They found no exposed outcrops of the reddish shale because the rock is so soft that if it does reach the surface, its layers soon weather away into unreadable mud. What the McCollums did discover was that workers on a sewage containment system had dug a series of holes on the south end of the lake, then dumped that material along the roadside on the rise.

The geologists took a small backhoe to the lakeside site and tried to dig down to the hidden steptoes, but a few trial attempts made it clear that major excavation would be necessary to expose any significant outcrops. Undaunted, the McCollums and a small group of EWU students patiently gathered promising chunks of shale from around telephone poles, rodent burrows and a single hand-dug pit. During further explorations in the same vicinity, the team found more trilobites in another layer exposed by a ditch, dug in 1904 and still in practical use.

❖ ❖ ❖

Laboratory study of the various shale samples revealed at least four species of trilobites, including *Glossopleura*. The geologists also discovered tiny sponge spicules and a range of small brachiopod fossils — phosphate-based shells related to modern lamp shells. These brachiopods lived as filter feeders that burrowed in the mud or attached to stationary objects in a shallow sea during the middle Cambrian Period, when the edge of our continent ended around the border of the Idaho panhandle.

Another group of marine animals called hyolithids left their impressions behind in the shale. Each hyolithid lived inside a cone-shaped shell topped with an operculum, or door, that could close them in for protection like a modern snail. The resulting imprint looks exactly like a small ice cream cone. Hyolithids were also filter feeders, but a pair of curious tentacle-like filaments the emerged from the operculum may have acted as stabilizers or oars to give them some range of mobility.

Animals such as trilobites and hyolithids, which have no direct modern descendants, add to the lure of the Cambrian Period for anyone who studies the past. More than half a billion years ago, the Cambrian marked the beginning of life as we know it, with ocean ancestors of every living form except flowering plants appearing in remarkable profusion. Many are elegantly preserved as fossils, and some of the best-known examples — such as the confounding hyolithids — have been described from the Burgess Shale formation in the Canadian Rockies, 300 miles north of Clear Lake. Thanks to an oil driller, ditch diggers, a septic holding system, busy gophers and some alert geologists, Spokane County has its own examples of these primordial creatures to ponder, too. ∎

The landscape around Palouse Falls shows evidence of the Missoula Floods.

CHIP PHILLIPS PHOTOGRAPHY

The Missoula Floods

BY NICHOLAS DESHAIS

First published in the *Inlander* on April 12, 2012

Get out of the car, hop over a few thin streams and a rock amphitheater appears, its tall walls winding around, almost forming a perfect circle in the Earth just south of Cheney, Washington.

Pillars of basalt cluster together forming high cliffs around the area, known as Williams Lake Cataract, but none of it will last. The cliff's edge is precarious, and a sloping hill of broken, shattered pillars pile up at its base. A wetland sits in the valley below.

At the edge of the stone arena, John Soennichsen scans the horizon like a man out of time.

It's not that he's in a rush. He just doesn't see this landscape as how it is now, barely after 9 on a Thursday morning that left an unseasonable covering of snow on the ground, with a cow peacefully lowing in the distance.

Instead, Soennichsen ("sun-ick-sun") sees something that happened thousands of years ago. A torrent of muddy water is rushing around him, its surface high above. Something akin to a tornado — one made of water — has planted itself in front of him, tearing at the ground, gouging deep into the Earth, making the amphitheater deeper and wider.

"We'd be at the bottom," he says. "The surface would have been 200 feet above us. From the air, this would have maybe looked like a ripple."

And this is just one spot, a few acres in an area stretching from Montana to the Pacific Coast that suffered a similar cataclysmic fate. Many areas saw much greater destruction.

Beginning at about the same time humans are thought to have first moved into the area, great floods washed over the Inland Northwest every 50 to 100 years, perhaps a hundred of them in all. These ice age floods washed away every living thing, scraped away fertile topsoil, carved out the Columbia River Gorge and forever changed the landscape of the Pacific Northwest. The floodwaters ran from Missoula, Montana, to the Pacific Ocean in a matter of weeks.

"Historically, no human has seen anything of this magnitude," says Richard Orndorff, the head of the geology department at Eastern Washington University. "These are the largest floods to occur anywhere on Earth that we know of."

For people like Orndorff and Soennichsen, it isn't what the floods washed away that fascinates them. It's what they left behind: giant gashes ripped in the Earth, waterfalls larger than Niagara with no water, mysterious pits in the ground big enough to hold a mansion, craggy buttes of basalt pillars, layer after layer of sediment that look to be left by a giant river where a giant river never ran. In all, it looks as if the Earth has scabbed over recently-torn flesh, mimicking something you'd see on Mars.

Soennichsen, who lives in Cheney, has become the local sage of sorts for looking into the region's geologic past and translating what happened for the lay audience. As the author of *Washington's Channeled Scablands Guide*, he's once again told the tale of what happened here in the age of the mammoth. A few years ago, he wrote *Bretz's Flood*, a well-received biography of J Harlan Bretz, the 20th century geologist who first recognized the signs of a humongous flood in the braided networks of coulees and erratically strewn boulders of Eastern and Central Washington.

Soennichsen is not a geologist by training, but a writer. He's just trying to tell a story.

"I worked at Eastern Washington University and befriended a lot of geologists," he says. "Unlike some scientists, they love to explain their work."

And as Soennichsen has pointed out many times — in his books, during his lectures — if you can read the landscape of Eastern Washington, you will hear the story of the floods.

Pushing the bounds of human comprehension, some stories about geology can begin with the words, "About a thousand million years ago…"

Not this one. When this one began about 15,000 years ago, the Earth's most recent ice age was ending. Dinosaurs were long gone, and the Earth's continents, creatures and plants were as recognizable as they are to us today. (Though we're missing a few giant animals that were around then: the 20-foot-tall giant sloth, the giant beaver, the mammoth and the sabre tooth tiger, to name a few.) There's a chance that people already called the Inland Northwest home.

Sheets of ice covered the planet's cooler regions, and these were beginning to retreat as the Earth warmed. As the Cordilleran ice sheet withdrew north, part of it blocked Montana's Clark Fork River. The river's waters continued to flow but had nowhere to go. Soon a lake 200 miles long and 2,000 feet deep sat behind this ice dam, covering present-day Missoula and its surroundings. Where Glacial Lake Missoula's waves crashed can still be seen on the hills surrounding the college town as unearthly horizontal ripples.

As the world's temperatures inched upwards, the ice dam melted and broke, sending an unimaginable amount of water rushing west, over Eastern and Central Washington, down the Gorge, up Oregon's Willamette Valley and into the Pacific Ocean. The lake, bigger than two of the nation's Great Lakes, drained within a few days.

Anyone unfortunate enough to be standing in Spokane the day the floods came would have seen a muddy torrent hundreds of feet tall rushing at 60 miles per hour enter the Spokane Valley from Rathdrum Prairie.

Deep waters submerged the Valley and Spokane, scouring the ground. The landmark knobs of black basalt that dot the region were unearthed by the floodwaters.

The cramped, icy mountain passageways the floodwaters took before entering Spokane didn't provide much fodder for destruction. Heading toward Cheney, the floodwaters found their first real chance to spread out and tear up the yielding ground, where at the time it is believed that a landscape similar to the fertile rolling hills of the Palouse stretched across Eastern Washington.

With no big river to follow, the floods made their own way. From high above, the path they took through Eastern and Central Washington looks like a complicated network of veins, braided channels that weave in and out of each other.

These are what University of Montana geologist David Alt calls "the classic, the granddaddy of all Scablands," in his book *Glacial Lake Missoula and its Humongous Floods*. And it is this area that Soennichsen's guidebook seeks to explain.

These are the channeled scablands, a broad expanse of interlaced gorges that cover much of this side of Washington. This carved out topography defines the area that we all know today.

"If we look at the general landscape, Eastern and Central Washington were scoured by these floods," says Orndorff, the EWU geologist. Name any feature on this side of the state, and the floods were probably responsible. Turnbull Wildlife Refuge, Grand Coulee, Soap Lake, the list goes on, Orndorff says. Even our drinking water.

"The Spokane Rathdrum Prairie Aquifer … is a sediment hosted aquifer," he says. "The sediment was deposited by those floods. … That's Montana sediment. That's why we have clean water."

Even our recreation.

"The floods created all of our lakes," Orndorff says. "We have so many lakes — 80 lakes basically within an hour of Spokane. Those were all carved out by these floods … torn out by these fast moving waters."

It's also a region that many people might find alien.

When the first detailed images of Mars came back in the 1970s from NASA's Viking orbiters, scientist V.R. Baker noted the similarity between the intertwined canyons on Mars and the scablands of Eastern Washington. This led many to speculate that what happened here happened there, that Eastern Washington's topography isn't simply Earthly, but also Martian.

❖ ❖ ❖

It didn't take sophisticated rocketry and planet hopping for J Harlan Bretz, a University of Chicago geologist, to recognize what forces created the area that the first pioneers dubbed the scablands.

Before he pursued his eventual vocation, Bretz was a high school biology teacher in Seattle. It was then, in 1910 at age 27, that he first became enamored with Eastern Washington.

After looking at a map of the Potholes Cataract near Moses Lake, Bretz thought it looked a large amount of water used to flow there, as if a massive waterfall once raged there.

"He no doubt asked people in the UW Geology Department about it," says Vic Baker, a geosciences professor at the University of Arizona, in *Bretz's Flood*. "And they probably said, 'Yes, you're right, that is interesting,' but offered no solutions to this curious high school teacher. But it clearly stuck in his mind as an odd thing, and it no doubt served as a trigger for later thinking."

A few years later, Bretz headed back to his native Midwest to pursue an advanced degree in geology at the University of Chicago. He wrote his dissertation on the glacial history of Puget Sound, but the scablands never left his thinking.

Every summer for seven years beginning in 1922, he came to Eastern Washington with some of his students to study the features in the landscape that had until then been poorly explained, if explained at all. The thinking at the time was that glaciers carved out the scablands. Bretz never really believed it.

During those summers, Bretz and his crew went to Williams, Badger, Fish and Rock lakes. They explored coulees with names like Moses, Washtucna and Grand. They poked around Drumheller Channels and Palouse Falls. From Spokane to Wenatchee, and from the Tri-Cities to the Grand Coulee (before it was dammed), Bretz and his students studied the broken landscape, collecting evidence of these destructive floods.

Within a year, Bretz had formulated a theory of the only thing that could have caused the scablands: catastrophic flooding. Bretz believed that what he discovered had happened nowhere else on Earth.

When he published *The Channeled Scablands of the Columbia Plateau* in 1923, his colleagues reacted in a way familiar to those who come up with innovative ideas and theories. They rejected it.

At the time, the field of geology was going through a stage of professional growth, trying hard to earn the respect of its peers. Unlike physicists and chemists, who had already changed the course of the world with their advances in the previous century, geologists were still trying to show that what they studied had real-world effects.

"Geology was at an age when it was trying to prove itself," says Soennichsen.

The field was deeply married to the theory of uniformitarianism, which assumed that laws governing the universe now have always governed the universe. In geology, this translated to a virtually unchanging earth, where gradual processes altered the landscape over millions of years.

"And here comes this guy saying it all happened in two weeks," Soennichsen says. Under the disapproving glare of his field's elders, Bretz tooled around the nation's outback with a hammer, resurrecting the idea of a great flood, just years after the geological scientific establishment had abandoned the biblical explanation of a great flood — Noah's — shaping the Earth.

"Ideas without precedent are generally looked upon with disfavor, and men are shocked if their conceptions of an orderly world are challenged," Bretz wrote of the feud in 1928.

"Not only was he claiming something most people didn't believe," Soennichsen says more plainly, "he was also an asshole."

Along with J.T. Pardee, the geologist who studied Glacial Lake Missoula, Bretz defended his flood theory for decades. It wasn't until the 1970s that his ideas were vindicated and accepted as truth.

In 1979, decades after his work in the channeled scablands, Bretz finally won the Penrose Medal of the Geological Society of America, geology's highest honor. His old age made him too frail to travel and accept the award, but he did tell his son, "All my enemies are dead, so I have no one to gloat over."

He died two years later.

❖ ❖ ❖

Leaving Eastern Washington's scablands, the floodwaters continued on their southwesterly course, crashing through the Wallula Gap, a high-walled narrow passage that bottlenecked the water before it rushed down the Columbia River Gorge.

Before the floods, the valley walls of the Gorge sloped gently downward to the river's banks. But as the water raged through, as deep as 1,000 feet in some sections of the Gorge, it tore at these sides. Where creeks once gently flowed downhill to join the Columbia, now they tumbled off steep cliffs. Multnomah Falls is but one well-known example.

Still massive and moving fast, the floods completely inundated Oregon's Willamette Valley. From Portland to Eugene, slackwater collected as narrow points near Portland kept it from racing out as fast as it raced in. Due to the stillness of the water, much of the soil stripped from Eastern Washington's plains was dropped here.

"It spreads the natural fertility of the Palouse Hills across the floor of the Willamette Valley," writes Alt in *Glacial Lake Missoula*. "Think of all the barren bedrock in the … scablands as you pass the lush fields and the flourishing groves of fruit and nut trees in the Willamette Valley."

What began high in the mountains of Montana finally came to end just two or three weeks later when the powerful floods reached the Pacific Coast, where the Columbia River meets the ocean. The greatest flood in Earth's history was done.

Fifty or so years later, it happened again. And again and again, perhaps up to 100 times for the next 5,000 years. In all, the floods covered 16,000 square miles, more than four times the size of Yellowstone National Park.

"That's the problem with the floods," says Mark Buser, president of the Ice Age Floods Institute, which is based in Kettle Falls, Washington. "People have a hard time wrapping their minds around the enormity of the floods. Everything is on such a grand scale. One flood had 10 times the flow of all the world's rivers, combined."

It's getting people to appreciate the enormity of the flood that is the institute's main goal. Founded in 1995, the institute has been trying to get the word out about the floods, which was generally known by the scientific community but wasn't a public story.

Since its inception, the institute has grown to 10 local chapters in four states, with 600 members. And it's not a "Geologists Only" organization. Buser, its president, is a financial advisor in the Portland area, focusing on tourism and economic development. Part of what fascinates him about what the institute has done, he says, is not just the science, but also the political science.

"I am fascinated by how citizens who appreciate the natural beauty of something can get a law through Congress," he says.

In 2009, the institute was instrumental in convincing Congress to establish the Ice Age Floods National Geologic Trail. Just two months into his presidency, Barack Obama signed the trail into reality. When complete, the trail will be the first of its kind to commemorate the country's natural history.

Unlike other national parks, the trail will be an independent unit of the National Park System. The federal agency will coordinate the planning and development of the trail, but the trail will be run by a collection of public and private organizations, most importantly the Ice Age Floods Institute.

This fall, the required "Foundation Statement" for the trail was released, detailing the major route of the trail and its many spurs. The main route stretches through four states from Missoula to Astoria, Oregon, with countless waypoints in between. The statement also identifies the significant points along the trail that should have interpretive centers, hiking trails and more.

"Think of a string of pearls," says Buser. "And the pearls are the most dramatic and beautiful sites, where it is most compelling to tell a story. Dry Falls, for example. … There are plans there for an extremely large interpretative center.

"The features so unique and abundant in the four states," Buser says. "They are nationally important, but they are also an international phenomena. They're known as the largest floods to ever occur on Earth."

❖ ❖ ❖

The clouds are dark and low seeming, and the wind is strong at the south end of Rock Lake, the only public access point for the eight-mile long waterway.

As Soennichsen pulls into the gravel parking lot, hundreds of geese and ducks take to the air, disturbed by the human intrusion in this otherwise placid place.

"It just doesn't feel right," he says of the lake, making no motion to step from his car.

Rock Lake is the longest and the deepest of the scabland lakes, and it's connected to Bonnie Lake in one long gash on the landscape just south of the Turnbull National Wildlife Refuge.

Basalt cliffs 300 feet tall line Rock Lake's edges, and they continue another 400 feet below the lake's surface. Sharp edged basalt columns wait just below the surface in some parts of the lake, ready to tear into the hull any boat with an unsuspecting oarsman.

In his Pulitzer Prize-winning *Annals of the Former World*, John McPhee argues that "writing about geology is masochistic, mind-fracturing self-enslaved labor." In his chapter on Rock Lake, which he calls the "eeriest of all scabland lakes," Soennichsen proves him wrong.

"Just about every facet of Rock Lake is entwined with mystery," he writes in the guidebook. "For centuries, Native Americans in the region have told stories of a sea serpent in the lake that would rip the bottoms out of … canoes and swallow the occupants. To this day, strange currents on

22

the surface of the lake ... only serve to sustain the legend."

Sadly just last week, the dangerous lake took another victim when Christopher James Gormley's kayak upended on the choppy waters. The 18-year-old Gonzaga University freshman was wearing a life jacket, but was pronounced dead from hypothermia at the hospital.

Not all of Rock Lake's stories are so tragic. There are rumors of an abandoned still in one of the caves near the lake, an artifact from the Prohibition era. And there's the story of the derailed train cars that plummeted into the lake 100 years ago, never to be found. They were packed with brand-new Ford Model T cars.

Pulling away from the lake, heading to yet another strange, severe feature left behind by the floods, Soennichsen allows himself to speculate on the nature of the floods.

"They say there's no reason why it wouldn't happen again," he says. "But we'll probably be long gone by then." ■

Woody Guthrie spent a month in Eastern Washington, writing songs for the BPA.

The Bard of Grand Coulee: Woody Guthrie

BY ROBERT CARRIKER

First published in the *Inlander* on July 3, 1996

The director of the Bonneville Power Administration didn't usually audition songwriters in his office, but he made an exception for Woody Guthrie. The 28-year-old writer and singer desperately needed a job, so for a solid hour he strummed his guitar, sang folk songs and generally entertained BPA's director, Paul Raver. What Raver heard that May morning in 1941 impressed him, so he rewarded the awkward young man from Los Angeles with a one-month BPA contract worth $266.66 to work as an "Information Consultant." Guthrie, in turn, obligated himself to write songs that would make people in the Pacific Northwest appreciate the work of the BPA and value the concept of public power.

Not everyone in the Pacific Northwest thought the BPA, or even its second giant dam on the Columbia River — the Grand Coulee — was a good idea. For the 15 years prior to 1933, when President Franklin D. Roosevelt finally approved construction of the BPA as part of the New Deal, a bitter debate had raged in central and Eastern Washington over the best location for a dam that would, first, back up water for irrigation and, second, produce electricity. Even after President Roosevelt settled the issue with his decision to place the dam at the head of Grand Coulee in the scablands of central Washington, few welcomed the prospect of a high dam on the middle Columbia River. The Spokane Chamber of Commerce and local press, both decidedly influenced by Washington Water Power, still favored private over public power.

Four years later, President Roosevelt dedicated Bonneville Dam in the Columbia River Gorge, but many citizens of Washington and Oregon still gave only grudging acknowledgment to the advantages of public power: cheap electricity, irrigation of desert land, navigation and flood control. Undeterred, Roosevelt created the Bonneville Power Administration to market the near-limitless electricity that would flow from any and all Columbia River dams. After Germany invaded Poland in 1939, the federal government declared Grand Coulee Dam a national defense project and its primary purpose became one of electricity, not irrigation.

That patriotic designation, however, still did not change many minds. In March of 1941, as Grand Coulee Dam neared completion, voters in Spokane, Portland, Eugene and Tacoma rejected the idea of switching to electrical lines connected to the BPA. Some people used terms like "Socialist boondoggle" to describe the public power concept. Clearly, BPA needed to illuminate the advantages of public power to the people of Washington and Oregon. Woody Guthrie had his work cut out for him.

❖ ❖ ❖

Following the administration of his oath of office on May 13, Woody embarked upon the most productive month of songwriting in his life. From outward appearances, it did not look to Stephen Kahn, BPA's acting chief of the information division, as if his new employee was capable of anything, much less swaying peoples' minds. Smallish in build, the wiry young man with the tipped-up nose and thin lips looked delicate — an impression accentuated by his tiny hands and feet. Rumpled clothes and kinky, uncombed black hair were Woody's only likeness to the rugged men who worked for the BPA, building mammoth concrete structures. But songwriting did not take muscles; it required brains and profound life experiences, something Guthrie had in abundance, and Kahn soon repented of his first impression.

In his single month of employment, Guthrie wrote 26 songs for the BPA, including anthems, talking blues and ballads. A half-century later, Kahn told a *New York Times* reporter, "In retrospect, I don't think the government has ever gotten a better investment on its money."

The original job description called for a homespun, folksy singer/narrator who could do voice-overs in a BPA documentary film called *The Columbia*. Kahn's first film production for the agency, *Hydro*, had come out the year before to lukewarm public reaction. It was, after all, thinly disguised government propaganda. The new film needed to appeal more to the proverbial "little guy," thus Kahn's decision to include folk songs. Kahn intended that the soundtrack songs later could be played from huge speakers at public power rallies.

It took only a single telephone call to locate the right man for the job. The archivist in charge of folk songs at the Library of Congress recommended Woody Guthrie. A recent veteran of work behind the microphone at CBS radio in New York, and a respected folk singer for his *Dust Bowl Ballads* album, he had already won Americans over with his popular song, "This Land Is Your Land." The director of Kahn's film, Gunther Von Fritsch, interviewed Woody in April in Los Angeles, but he was not as confident about the producer's choice. "I could see he had the kind of talent I was looking for," Von Fritsch said, "but I hadn't made up my mind." Maybe Von Fritsch had heard rumors of Woody's poor work record, his irascibility and his utter refusal to accept responsibility, even for his wife and three children.

❖ ❖ ❖

Living, not working, was Woody Guthrie's great talent. Born in Okemah, Oklahoma, in 1912, he resided in Pampa, Texas, during the Dust Bowl years. A never-ending search for jobs took him from Ohio to California during the 1930s. Years of riding the rails gave him no specific work skills, but it did make him a songwriter and a singer. He always traveled with his guitar, and inevitably someone in the boxcar or the hobo jungle would urge him to sing a song he remembered from the days when families still had farms. He could learn it from them and then sing it better than his teachers. Three things happened to Woody: he learned a variety of folk song styles, from the Appalachians to the Ozarks; he began to make up his own lyrics, improvising to make his message more appropriate to his location and audience; and Woody realized that music has a profound impact on the way people think, because they concentrate on lyrics to a much greater degree than the words in speeches or books.

Woody arrived in Hollywood in 1937 a displaced Okie and vagrant, but he left three years later a radio personality. It was the heyday of the singing cowboy, and Woody Guthrie fit in almost as easily as Gene Autry and Roy Rogers once he persuaded station KFVD to give him some air time. He made the most of the opportunity to promote not only his singing talent and Will Rogers-like wit but also his liberal political views. Though Woody never enrolled as a member, the American Communist Party became one of his biggest supporters, especially after the publication of John Steinbeck's *The Grapes of Wrath* called attention to the same injustices Woody sang about on the radio.

In 1939, Woody, on a lark, invited himself to be the Los Angeles columnist for the party's San Francisco newspaper, *The Daily People's World*. New York beckoned soon thereafter, and for a year Woody, now reunited with his family, enjoyed the luxury of celebrity status as the star of the Model Tobacco's show, "Pipe Smoking Time." Impulsively, the morning after New Year's Day, 1941, Woody got himself fired in New York. He probably just wanted to return to California. Perhaps he also didn't like what he had become: a well-paid performer who sang militant songs about social injustice.

California had changed. The Okies who had come West with him in 1937 were now happily employed in wartime industries. His old job on KFVD was not waiting for him, a finance company threatened to repossess his family's new Pontiac and Mary Guthrie contemplated divorce. Heavy drinking lessened Woody's daily pain. It is easy to see why Von Fritsch wanted to consider others.

Woody, however, needed the work, so he piled Mary and the children into the Pontiac and drove to Portland. Funding for the film had been temporarily delayed, as Woody found out when he arrived, but BPA head Raver liked him, so he got the job anyway. Obviously, no one at the BPA regularly read *The People's Daily World*, or Woody's journey would have been in vain.

❖ ❖ ❖

After the repo man looking for Woody's Pontiac tracked him down in Portland, Von Fritsch arranged for Elmer Buehler to drive Guthrie around Washington State in a 1940 Hudson. Woody himself said he saw the "Columbia River and the big Grand Coulee Dam from just about every cliff, mountain, tree and post from which it could be seen."

He also visited logging camps, farms, skid rows and granges. 'The poor guy had BO [body odor] so bad you could hardly stand it," Buehler remembered, adding that "a lot of people just couldn't."

But when he unlimbered his voice and guitar, the Professional Okie, as Woody often referred to himself, touched the hearts of working people in the Pacific Northwest. He made up songs about powder monkeys, lumberjacks, jackhammer men, hobos, farmers and migrants — the people who made up the work force in rural Washington.

Information chief Kahn demanded that Woody produce three pages of songs each day, "like in Hollywood," he said, "where they require a script writer to turn out three pages a day, or something you know, no matter how good or bad it is." As a result, Woody sometimes threw in songs he had written before, or he just changed a few lines. Sometimes he just scribbled down lyrics, neglecting to supply a tune. (Not until the 1980s did folk singer Pete Seeger match all of Woody's lyrics to tunes.) At other times, he attached new words to old, familiar folk baselines, which allowed Woody's listeners to concentrate on his new stanzas, because they already knew the music.

Woody's signature song in the Pacific Northwest became "Roll on, Columbia," and it, for example, uses a chorus from "Goodnight, Irene," the classic authored by Huddie Ledbetter, or Leadbelly as he is known to the ages. Similarly, Woody borrowed from "Old Smokie," "Pretty Polly," "Muleskinner's Blues" and others. Folk singing is, after all, a process. But when he felt completely original, Woody said he liked to "knock off two or three pretty fair songs a week and a pretty darn good one over the weekend." Music, he volunteered, "is some kind of electricity that makes a radio out of a man, and the dial is in his head and he just sings according to how he's a feeling."

❖ ❖ ❖

There is no doubt that Woody deeply loved what he called the mineral mountains, chemical deserts, rough canyons and sawblade snowcaps of the Pacific Northwest. Moreover, he believed in what he wrote and sang about Grand Coulee Dam, considering it a "necessary humanitarian experiment." To him the dam stood as a monument of working-class consciousness and solidarity. Still, when his month was over in mid-June,

Woody gladly returned to New York, where he scratched the words "This Machine Kills Fascists" on his guitar and ferreted out new opportunities.

Before he left Portland, Woody recorded 11 of his new songs on acetate disks for the BPA. Alan Lomax of the Library of Congress describes the historic cuts this way: "The moans and howls and mutters of his harmonica combine the sounds of a lonesome freight train whistle and a semi's klaxon. The vibrant underbelly is Woody's hard-driving Carter family lick on his guitar; the left hand constantly hammering on, pulling off and sliding to create all sorts of syncopations in the bass runs and melody, the right hand flailing with a very flexible pick to make rhythmic rattles and rustles and bumps such as a hobo hears in a freight car or a hitch-hiker feels in the cabin of a big cross-country trailer."

Only three of Woody's songs made it into the soundtrack of *The Columbia*. Budget problems caused by World War II delayed the film's completion until 1948, and by then no one needed songs and celluloid to describe the impact of the BPA in the Pacific Northwest. In 1953, a new Republican administration ordered all copies of *The Columbia* and its songs destroyed when it learned of Guthrie's Communist Party connections. As a result, Woody's Pacific Northwest documents consist mostly of copies and the acetate disks.

But these are enough. Woody's work songs about Jackhammer John and "The Biggest Thing That Man Has Ever Done" are still sung today wherever folklorists gather. In 1987 the state legislature named "Roll on, Columbia" the official Washington state folk song. A whole generation of songwriters, including Bob Dylan, Joni Mitchell and Bruce Springsteen, consider Woody Guthrie their special inspiration.

Joe Klein's superb biography Woody Guthrie, *A Life*, argues that Guthrie's stature derives from the fact that he had something to say and he said it in songs that could be sung by anyone. A mediocre guitarist and a technically limited singer, Woody used the typewriter as his most effective instrument, Klein writes.

Rolling Stone magazine agrees. It speculates that, had Woody not died in 1967, he would be heavily into rap today because he always loved words better than music. And what words would he be singing? Spokane native Bill Murlin, the BPA officer who assembled all 26 of Guthrie's 1941 song sheets and records, told the *New York Times* on the 50th anniversary of the Bonneville Power Administration: "If we hired Woody Guthrie today, we'd have him singing about saving salmon and conserving energy, instead of using him to sell power." ∎

While no visual record of Spokane House exists, this 1998 recreation
for the *Inlander* reflects what is known about the structure.

INLANDER COVER ILLUSTRATION / IVAN MUNK

Life at Spokane House

BY JACK NISBET

First published in the *Inlander* on June 17, 2010

The time was probably early summer of 1810 when a small group of strangers rode into the Spokane village on the flat point of land at the confluence of the Spokane and Little Spokane rivers. Summer salmon runs would have just begun, drawing families from many Plateau tribes to their traditional fishing camps. A wickerwork weir that jutted into the Spokane River diverted some of the salmon into eddies, where the men could spear them in great numbers; another weir stretched across the entire width of the Little Spokane. Women split the catch, then hung the red-fleshed halves on wooden racks to dry. The smell of salmon oil and the buzz of yellow jackets would have mixed with stick game songs in a variety of languages amid dust kicked up by ancient dances. The Spokanes called the confluence of the two rivers "the gathering place."

No surviving account describes the arrival of these newcomers, but they had started from Lake Pend Oreille. Their leader, Jacques Raphael Finlay, was employed by the North West Company, a fur-trading conglomerate based in Montreal that was expanding into the Inland Northwest. Jaco and his small crew of French-Canadian *voyageurs* came bearing trade items such as tobacco, kettles, knives, wool cloth and fish hooks. They were the first white men most members of the Spokane Tribe had ever seen.

In the 12 years they spent at the confluence — just north of the modern-day Nine Mile Dam — these men would mesh in important ways with local tribal culture, often wedding tribal women. They had a hand in sending Spokane Garry — the middle Spokane chief who would spend his life trying to keep the peace between tribes and later settlers — off to Protestant boarding school. And though their presence was short-lived, compared with how long the Spokanes had been at *Nin Chin Tseen* — the Great Gathering Place — their impact is still felt today.

❖ ❖ ❖

Long before Finlay arrived at their village, the Spokanes had felt the presence of Europeans. Spanish horses had reached the Plateau tribes at least half a century earlier; according to tribal tradition, the Spokanes traded their first animals from the Nez Perce. The horses thrived in the open pine prairies among the nutritious bunchgrass, but even as Spokane families built up their herds, they would have known that the source of this new wealth could not be far behind. Tribal oral accounts tell of visiting Kootenais, who escorted two French trappers into the area around 1800. The white men, whose balding heads and bushy beards sparked raucous laughter, were short of food, so the Spokanes fed them and gave them clothes. The men purchased furs and supposedly wintered in the Colville Valley before returning to the north.

A few years later, hearing of other white men to the south, the Spokanes dispatched two runners to the Snake River, where they met Lewis and Clark's Corps of Discovery and returned with a looking glass to show their families. After one more winter, stories filtered into the area of more fur traders in the Kootenai country. This was the party of North West Fur Company agent David Thompson, who crossed the Divide in 1807. During the next two years, Thompson built three trade houses in the drainages north of Spokane: Kootanae House at the source lakes of the Columbia; Kullyspel House on Lake Pend Oreille; and Saleesh House on the Clark Fork River.In the fall of 1809, four Spokane men made an excursion to meet Thompson at a Kalispel encampment near modern Cusick on the Pend Oreille River, carrying gifts of a horse and several muskrat pelts. Thompson would have asked the Spokane emissaries about the geography and fur prospects of their homeland, and their answers must have convinced him to establish an outpost in their neighborhood, for in early May 1810, he gave his clerk Jaco Finlay "summer orders" that apparently involved the Spokane country.

❖ ❖ ❖

The son of a Scottish fur trader and a Cree mother, 42-year-old Jaco Finlay had worked most of his career in the Canadian Prairies as a clerk, interpreter and independent trapper. Beginning in 1806, he had scouted for the North West Company's thrust across the Rocky Mountains. At the confluence of the two Spokane rivers, Finlay would have recognized that the variety of people and the trails converging from all directions created an ideal situation for a trade house. There was plentiful fish for food, horses to trade, bunchgrass for fodder and wood for building and fires. Undoubtedly relying on tribal advice and approval, he chose a site and set his crew to building the first white settlement in present-day Washington.

Spokane elder Louie Wildshoe later recalled that his mother-in-law was a little girl when the first fur trade post was built at the confluence. She told him that the white people spoke French, and that they located their post halfway between the two rivers, near a long-established tribal village.

Jaco's North West Company crew would have built many trade houses over the years, using one basic design: Three structures — men's quarters, a warehouse and a store — were arranged in a U shape. According to Spokane tradition, the white men planted potatoes in their gardens; they also ate horse and dog meat. The whites traded with Spokane bands: flint and fire-starting steels; knives, axes and guns; pots and metal utensils; calico cloth and wool blankets.

Soon, Jaco Finlay was living with a Spokane wife called Teshwintichina and had apparently settled in to a lifestyle that combined aspects of Plateau and fur trade culture. Their first child, a daughter later baptized as Marie Josephte, was born at the post.

At some point during the next year, Jaco was joined by another of David Thompson's clerks, a strapping red-haired Scot named Finan McDonald. Assigned to man the company's Saleesh House on the Clark Fork River, Finan had joined a group of Flathead and Kalispel hunters bound for the buffalo country east of the Rockies in the summer of 1810. There he took part in a skirmish with territorial Blackfeet that resulted in several casualties. Fearful of reprisals, McDonald and his voyageurs rode east to Finlay's new post. Thirty years old, full of both wild temper and good humor, McDonald traveled with a Kalispel wife he called Peggy and a young child.

Spokane House did not enter written history until chief agent David Thompson arrived there on June 14, 1811. He surveyed the pleasant flat of orange-barked ponderosa pine and made a brief entry in his field journal: "Thank Heaven for our good safe journey, here we found Jaco &c with ab[ou]t 40 Spokane families." Since Thompson estimated seven or eight people in each family, his census indicated a village with about 300 inhabitants. The next morning, Thompson produced his sextant and set about determining the latitude (47° 47' 4" N) and longitude (117° 27' 11" W) of the new post. After spending a day arranging the trade goods he had brought from eastern Canada (including two yards of wool cloth earmarked for Finlay) and trading for sucker fish and roots from the Spokanes, the surveyor headed north toward Kettle Falls to launch his historic run down the Columbia River to the sea.

On the return trip the following spring, David Thompson made another brief stop at Spokane House. He feasted on fresh steelhead, then proceeded through the Colville Valley and up the Columbia. After crossing the Rockies and continuing on to Montreal, he used his meticulous observations to draw a series of large maps that detailed North America from Hudson Bay to the Pacific. These charts contained the first accurate depictions of the Spokane River, which he called the Skeetshoo, and the Little Spokane (Weir Brook). He also dotted in the network of tribal trails that led to the rivers' confluence, where he carefully labeled "N.W Co. Spokane House."

❖ ❖ ❖

For an entire year after Thompson's departure, the North West Company enjoyed a monopoly on the fur trade at Spokane House and her subsidiary posts among Salish and Kootenai tribes. But competition was moving upstream in the guise of the Pacific Fur Company, founded by entrepreneur John Jacob Astor of New York City. The Americans had established Fort Astoria at the mouth of the Columbia and a post at the mouth of the Okanogan River in 1811. In August 1812, Astorian partner John Clarke led a party inland to compete directly with the Nor'Westers. Following a practice common among Canadian fur companies, Clarke chose a site in close proximity to Spokane House. By the onset of winter, the Astorians had constructed a four-room dwelling house for the "gentlemen," a comfortable bunkhouse for the workers, and a capacious store for the furs and trading goods. Although the Nor'westers had always enjoyed amiable relations with the tribes who frequented the area, Clarke erected a pole stockade around his new post, with two corner bastions for defense.

Alfred Seton, a young American who was stationed at an outpost on the Clearwater River, arrived for a visit with the Spokane Astorians in October 1812. Hungry, cold and tired after an arduous trip, he wrote that Mr. Clarke "received me very kindly & treated me to the best his house afforded, which was but Horse." Noting that the Astorians had already accumulated 15 packs (more than one-half ton) of beaver pelts during their short tenure, he observed that "the N. W. Co. did not much like the idea of our opposing them." Another visiting clerk wrote of the "sly and underhanded dealings" between the posts, both parties making "the amplest protestations of friendship and kindness" all the while maneuvering to capture the most trade. To their credit, the managing partners of the competing companies agreed that they would not trade "spirituous liquors" to the tribes.

By late fall in 1812, Clarke's "Spokan Fort" seemed on track for success. Then, sometime around Thanksgiving, the Nor'Westers' fall supply run from eastern Canada arrived with the news that the United States had declared war on Great Britain the previous June, and that a British warship was en route for the Columbia. After a Pacific Fur Company messenger carried word downriver to Astoria, a cloud of uncertainty descended over the whole Astorian enterprise. The Americans realized that their small fort at the mouth of the Columbia would be defenseless in the face of the Royal Navy. After several rounds of negotiations, the Pacific Fur Company sold their inventory to the North West Company and prepared to return east, with the understanding that any of Astor's employees who wished could transfer to the Canadian company.

In November 1813, the Nor'Westers moved their stock from their original house to the more expansive Spokan Fort. A young Irish clerk named Ross Cox found life at the Spokane headquarters quite agreeable. During the winter months, the river provided tasty sucker fish for sustenance, and spring steelhead were followed by rich runs of Chinook salmon; according to Cox, the residents "breakfasted on fish and dined on horse." The traders planted a large garden of turnips, potatoes, cabbages, melons, and cucumbers. In the summer of 1814, *bateaux* ferried a rooster, three hens, three goats and three hogs upriver from Astoria. Someone captured a bear cub and housed it in the pig sty. There it was "fed daily by one of our Canadians, of whom he became very fond, and who in a short time taught him to dance, beg, and play many tricks, which delighted the Indians exceedingly."

Summer at the post, Cox wrote, was occupied with "hunting, fishing, fowling, horse-racing and fruit-gathering; while reading, music, backgammon &c. formed the evening pleasures of our small but friendly mess." Spokane House became known as a delightful place, a "centre of attraction" with handsome buildings and fine horses that the traders delighted in racing against Indian ponies on a nearby flat. Ross Cox described meeting the headman of the Middle Spokane band, known to the whites as *Ilum-spokanee*, and visited their nearby village, noting that "some houses were oblong, others conical, and were covered with mats or skins, according to the wealth of the proprietor." He learned of the ongoing barter for horses between the Spokanes and the Nez Perce Tribe while remarking that the Spokanes would never kill a horse for their own food, although they supplied animals for the fur traders' table.

❖   ❖   ❖

In 1821, the North West Company merged with their primary rival, the Hudson's Bay Company, headquartered in London. At first, little changed at Spokane House. A single surviving post journal, kept by Finan McDonald and another clerk from April 1822 to April 1823, provides a detailed look at everyday life at the post. A stream of different Plateau tribes visited from across the region. Relationships between these native people and the fur men were almost always amicable, and the gates to the stockade were only shut for a single night during that entire span. Many of the clerks and workers were married to Plateau women, who helped tend the gardens and prepare fish and hides.

The traders and the Spokane Tribe operated separate fishing weirs, and the tribal fishermen always seemed to catch more salmon, trout, steelhead and suckers in theirs. In one of the only tense moments recorded in the journal, a hot-tempered Finan McDonald wrecked the canoe of a Spokane man who dared to spear fish below the company weir. The canoe owner responded by tearing down a section of fence around Finan's potato garden before cooler heads prevailed.

During the summer of 1822, workers at the post were busy with a major remodel of the 10-year-old buildings, including a new boathouse and defensive measures. But the following fall, when Nicholas Garry, governor of Hudson's Bay Company, visited Spokane House, he was not happy with the lifestyle he observed there: "The good people of Spokane District generally have shown an extraordinary predilection for European provisions without considering the enormous price it costs… They may be said to have been eating Gold," Garry wrote.

The next spring, after a consultation with Finan McDonald and other clerks, the governor decided to abandon the newly remodeled post and move its operations to a new location at Kettle Falls, to be called Fort Colvile. The logic was clear: The move would place the district headquarters on the Columbia's main stem and eliminate costly horse brigades to the mouth of the Spokane; the salmon at the Kettle Falls were even more abundant than those at Spokane House; outposts in the Kootenai and Flathead country could be easily supplied. The only difficulty the governor saw in taking leave of Spokane House was that "it may give offence to the Spokan Indians who have always been staunch to the Whites."

Before departing, the governor obtained permission from *Ilum-spokanee* to carry his young son east to attend school at the Red River Colony (near modern Winnipeg, Manitoba), in order to help the transition of the Spokane people into the modern world. The youngster was baptized with the name of Spokane Garry. When the fur brigade left that spring, the lad was tucked in among the season's fur packs, bound for eastern Canada.

By the spring of 1826, most of the trade goods and equipment had been ferried to the new Fort Colvile. The blacksmith and cook were collecting the last bits of iron from the place, right down to the door hinges. The clerk in charge of the move from Spokane commented that "the Indians much regret our going off," but when he returned during the summer fishing season, he found most of the people working at their traditional fishing barrier — and taking in 700 or 800 salmon per day.

The abandoned Spokane House buildings were apparently bequeathed to Jaco Finlay. Over the next two years, Jaco, Teshwintichina and a variety of offspring greeted numerous visitors traveling along the trails near the post. Jaco died in spring 1828 at the age of 60. According to tribal accounts, he and his effects were buried beneath a bastion at the corner of the old stockade.

Eight years later, when a Protestant missionary stopped by the site, he reported "a very pleasant, open valley, though not extensively wide. The North-west Company had a trading post here, one bastion of which is still standing." Apart from that single bastion, the confluence must have looked much as it had when Jaco first rode into the cluster of tule mat lodges in 1810.

❖ ❖ ❖

When a new wave of white settlers began building the city of Spokane in the 1870s, many made the trek nine miles downstream to survey the old Spokane House site, and pioneer reminiscences and tribal oral histories about the fur trade era surfaced regularly in local newspapers. For three years beginning in 1950, archaeological explorations on the site confirmed some of that history. During the second year of research, the diggers — working on a tip from a local historian who had listened to tribal stories — uncovered a bastion on the northwest corner of the old post's footprint. Beneath the square, the crew found a rotted coffin that contained human bones as well as a comb, a tin drinking mug, a hunting knife, part of a writing slate, three brass buttons, a pair of reading spectacles and five smoking pipes — one of them incised with the initials JF. The remains were declared to be those of Jaco Finlay, and were reinterred in 1976.

Today, a memorial brass plaque marking Jaco Finlay's grave is surrounded by colored steel beams delineating the outlines of the posts built in 1812 by the Pacific Fur Company and later enlarged and remodeled by the North West and Hudson's Bay Companies. The exact location of the original small trade house constructed by Jaco Finlay in the summer of 1810 has never been definitely determined.

Perhaps, however, the legacy of that first Spokane House lies not so much in its precise location as in its human impact. A large number of current citizens across the region count the men on the payrolls of the North West, Pacific Fur and Hudson's Bay Company as their ancestors. In a very real sense, Jaco Finlay, Finan McDonald and their Spokane House cohorts marked the beginning of the Inland Northwest we know today. ■

Spokane Garry was sent to Manitoba to learn in a white missionary school when he was 14 years old.

The Good Indian: Spokane Garry

BY KEVIN TAYLOR

First published in the *Inlander* on Sept. 25, 2008

"I had two hearts and have had two hearts ever since."

This is the heart of a quote from a man who was thrust by fate into the gristmill of change when two races, two cultures, two wildly disparate ways of living on Earth ground against each other like millstones right here in Spokane.

And with two hearts, well, there's twice the loss.

In a city that doesn't often recognize its indigenous past, a conflicted Spokane Indian who was born nearly 200 years ago stands at the crossroads of race relations yet again.

When a statue erected in honor of Spokane Garry was jack-hammered to the ground and hauled away to a dump earlier this year, Indians around town reacted sharply.

The statue had been repeatedly vandalized and damaged by weather over the years. But the sense of anger grew as it became clear the city had no plans to seek a replacement artwork of Garry and instead erected on his previous spot an abstract sculpture of a totem pole it got for free from the Northwest Museum of Arts and Culture.

That the sculptor was white added a little more sting, a number of Indians have said. The sculptor, David Govedare, joined his voice to the chorus of displeasure, telling the *Inlander* that he was never told his piece,

"Totem Ascension," was going to be used in such a manner, adding that it was hardly appropriate in Chief Garry Park.

The furor caught the attention of an 8-year-old girl who had just written a report on Garry for her third-grade history class. Victoria Schauer wrote a letter to the mayor that said, in part, "It makes me sad how he [Garry] was treated and I think we need to have a new and improved statue of him in his park and more mention of him throughout Spokane."

She put the letter in an envelope along with $5 of her allowance money and sent it to City Hall to start a fund for a new statue. As for her wish for more mention throughout Spokane…

"Indians are invisible in Spokane, still invisible," says author Sherman Alexie, a Spokane (and Coeur d'Alene) tribal member who grew up on the Spokane Indian Reservation at Wellpinit.

Charlene Teters, like Alexie, is a Spokane tribal member and an artist. She has taught at universities around the country and now is on the faculty of the Institute of American Indian Art in Santa Fe, New Mexico. When she was growing up in the city, "I remember at Shadle I was one of only two Indians in the school — and the other was my brother."

"It was like we were secrets," she says. "People would try to guess, 'Are you Italian? Are you Japanese?' They usually never guessed Indians. It never dawned on them that we were still around."

Schauer's donation sparked the creation of a committee appointed by Spokane Mayor Mary Verner to discuss a new Garry artwork. Her gesture also came to the attention of Jon Osterberg in Seattle, a media relations executive with Pemco Insurance and a history buff familiar with Garry. Osterberg convinced company executives to kick in $15,000 as seed money to help raise funds for a new statue or a bronze bust.

The *Inlander* has been seeking ideas for a Garry piece from several notable artists in the area. Strikingly, all three submitted by Indian artists are not representational at all, but speak instead to the culture.

One design includes the word "Indian" in steel. "It's just the idea that hey, we're here, you know? And you have to drive by the word Indian every day," artist Ric Gendron says of his design.

"Every time I go home, I go back into invisibility," Teters says. "I sort of joke that most people there don't know there are Spokane Indians who are not the baseball team."

In the manner of the Cheshire Cat, the question hangs hazily before us: Who was Garry? How do we find him through all the different lenses and distortions with which we view the past?

For example, George Simpson of the Hudson's Bay Company recalls seeing Garry in 1841, a decade after his Christian education at a fur company mission.

He was appalled, Simpson writes, to see Garry playing cards, eagerly thumbing "the black and greasy pasteboard … relapsed into his original barbarism."

A more likely view, retorts Jeanne Givens, a great-great-great granddaughter of Garry's who now lives in Bellevue: "He was being an Indian. Gambling and having fun is real Indian.

"I think Garry had to walk such a fine line. In order to be effective [keeping peace and negotiating for a homeland] he had to remain Indian," Givens adds.

So once again, 116 years after he died, Garry stands at the junction of indigenous and Western cultures, connecting the back then and the right now in a way he would never have imagined. Ultimately, should the new artwork represent him or his people?

❖ ❖ ❖

Spokane Garry had a life like a roller coaster with plenty of ups and downs. His death has been like that, too.

He was once a pivotal figure in treaty talks with governors, generals and other dignitaries stopping by to chat him up or have a cup of coffee. (He always had coffee beans and sugar on hand.)

By the time he was 81, however, Garry's star had faded and he was shriveling away in a tipi pitched in Indian Canyon, "pining away on his couch of skins," a newspaper wrote, where he died at 1 in the morning on January 13, 1892, according to his death return, which lists the cause of death as "congestion of the lungs."

So even his ornate headstone (donated by the Daughters of the American Revolution in 1925) is wrong, giving the date of his death as Jan. 12.

Garry's funeral and burial in a pauper's grave was held Jan. 16, according to the Jan. 15 editions of *The Spokesman*, which appears to have the most accurate account among local newspapers of the day.

Garry died on a day like many January days in Spokane — cold, dismal and likely overcast. National Weather Service records indicate he died in the middle of cold snap with snowfall.

The weather broke on the 15th, temperatures rising to 37 degrees, and his funeral was written up as something of a spectacle:

"Old Garry is Dead," cries the headline, "Gone to the Happy Hunting Grounds of the Great Beyond." The article says, "nearly all the members of the now-meager tribe were present," along with "a number of ladies and gentlemen of the paleface race."

All were heart-struck, it seems, when Garry's aged and blind widow, Nina, "was led up to the coffin and as she passed her hands over the familiar features and smoothed the long, gray hair for the last time tears coursed down her cheeks."

Garry didn't draw much praise from city fathers who, one thinks, would have appreciated Garry's steadfast work to keep relations between settlers and Indians friendly.

"An old skulker and a hypocrite," scoffed city of Spokane founder James N. Glover.

"He was weak and vacillating," added the Rev. H.T. Cowley.

Blessed are peacemakers. Even the one-armed moral crusader and Civil War Gen. O.O. Howard, who commanded the military's Department of the Columbia in the 1870s, had little good to say of Garry.

In his book, *Famous Indian Chiefs I Have Known*, Howard gushes about another Spokane leader, Lot, whom he describes as a "fine, tall Indian chief." Garry, he writes, "was a small, pompous, querulous old man, not at all like Lot."

❖ ❖ ❖

It wasn't always so. Garry was once considered the best and the brightest — a teenager sent by his people more than 1,000 miles from home to learn everything he could about whites.

His father, Ilum-spokanee, was a leader of the Middle Spokane, who lived mostly around the confluence of the Spokane and Little Spokane rivers. (Upper Spokane lived upstream at the present-day city and parts of the Valley. Lower Spokane lived downriver, where the reservation is today.)

Garry was born about 1811, just a few years after fur traders began nosing around the area. By the time Garry was 14, competing fur trading companies and area tribes were engaged in serious deal making.

Hudson's Bay Company representatives called a meeting with Ilum-spokanee and other Indian leaders at their trading outpost, Spokan House, in 1825 with a proposal that the tribes each pick a child to be educated in European ways at the Red River Mission in Winnipeg, Manitoba.

It's hard to say why popular historical writings are always so treacle-y, painting this as Indians going off to seek the "white man's medicine," as if they were a bunch of primitives who thought praying to a new god would cause metal goods to fall from the sky like manna.

It seems clear, from reading accounts of the time, that this was a pretty strategic business deal all around — the better the two parties could communicate, the better the dealings.

Still the Hudson's Bay people were taken aback when Ilum-spokanee chose his own son, as did a Kootenai leader. There was an ulp! moment (found in HBC correspondence) that no harm better come to these lads or there'd be hell to pay.

❖ ❖ ❖

Here's one of the sad things about Garry. We don't know his birth name. Also, family members told historian E.T. Becher in the 1950s that even his mission name was pronounced *jerry*, which, now that there is no voice to say it and only a word to look at, is lost also.

At Red River, officials renamed their Inland Northwest students (there were seven, eventually) with their tribe as one name and a company bigwig as another. So Garry became Spokane Garry and his companion became Kootenai Pelly, named for HBC governors.

Much has been written about Garry's five years of schooling, so imagine instead what it must have been like to come riding home for good in 1830 dressed in European clothing and a tam-o-shanter on his head. (Garry apparently loved the tam because one was still on his head when he was sketched by Gustavus Sohon in May 1855.) He was also fluent in French and English — the languages of both sets of newcomers exploring his homeland — and further, he could read and write and carried with him Bibles, prayer books and journals.

The import of Garry's literacy was potent and appears to have spread around the Inland Northwest like wildfire.

Historian Cecil Drury, in remarks to a Spokane history club in 1973, called Garry's Bible, "One of the most important books in the history of the Northwest." Not so much for the Word of God (although Drury may disagree), but more for the power of the written word Indians recognized as the key to dealing with whites. And Garry had cracked the code.

Drury told his audience a story that Lawyer, one of the pivotal leaders of the Nez Perce, immediately sought out Garry to have him read from the Bible. The meeting led to one of the critical incidents in cultural relations here. Four Nez Perce were dispatched on an epic journey to the east. They walked into St. Louis in 1831 looking for a General Clark — yes the Lewis-and-Clark Clark, whom the tribe had famously met in 1805 — and asked for missionaries to be sent this way. It seems they were really looking for teachers, but teachers and missionaries were often one and the same. Missionaries, both American Board Protestants and Jesuit Catholics, soon raced this way.

Ilum-spokanee had died in 1828 while Garry was away, but the son carried out the task he was given. Garry is credited with creating the first school in what was then called Oregon Territory, setting up a large structure of lodge poles and tule mats in what is now Drumheller Springs Park at Maple and Euclid. For years, mainly in winter when food gathering was slow, he taught both children and adults the ABCs, simple phrases from a Salish-English dictionary he created in his journals and how people could write their names.

He was also a fairly devout Episcopalian, enough so that when the missionaries reached here they found people who observed the Sabbath with Bible preaching and gospel hymns.

❖ ❖ ❖

Garry soon became a pretty prominent guy, enjoying the best of his two-hearts world. He had two wives and plenty of horses, signifying stature on his Indian side. He lived with white-guy comforts of Western clothing, some of the best technology available in his day, and goodly supplies of flour, sugar and coffee. He always rode a white horse.

By the 1850s, however, these dual aspects of Garry, instead of being double the fun, were going to pull him in two.

Settlement was increasing, gold had been discovered near Colville, and tensions were rising between one culture that roamed the land looking for such treasures as camas bulbs and another that dug up precious metals and chopped down trees.

Garry was such a notable that Gov. Isaac Stevens, on his way west as the first governor of the newly created Washington Territory, stopped by Garry's house on Oct. 17, 1853, to introduce himself. The two had a pleasant time conversing in both French and English, but were also, documents show, sizing each other up pretty carefully.

Garry, it is said, stayed hidden at a distance and watched Stevens for several hours before riding up to "discover" he had company. Stevens, despite writing cheery accounts of Garry's language and farming skills (wheat, potatoes, pumpkins, corn and squash) also wrote in his diary, "[He] is not frank, and I do not understand him."

Clearly, Garry was not the easily manipulated "savage" Stevens may have expected. Both men knew big changes were coming and neither wanted to tip his hand, it appears.

In fact, Garry references this in the postscript to a letter he wrote to Stevens a few years later, dated Sept. 12, 1856. The language is stunningly modern, as if it were speaking today: "P. S. Sir I have heard that you had said that the first time you would see me you were going to cut my balls out but I should not like it much and my old woman much less."

Bang! A quip that reveals Garry totally understood Stevens on a political level and had a deft sense of humor about it. And that Stevens didn't get the upper hand at that first meeting.

The body of the letter further expands the sense that Garry and Stevens had a clear understanding of each other. Garry writes that Stevens has chosen a bad time for a treaty talk — salmon were running at the Spokane Falls, and his people were laying in their winter's supply. Plus, almost all the Coeur d'Alene had gone across the Rocky Mountains to hunt buffalo, similarly gathering food for winter.

He acknowledges hearing unsettling rumors of war and of Stevens "talking hard" about Indians but adds, "you have more confidence in me than that … for I know you know too much to give credit to such idle talk. When we next meet we can have a good understanding together for I will keep nothing from you and expect the same from you."

❖ ❖ ❖

Little more than a year after that letter, Garry was on the cusp of his downfall. Tensions kept rising. Indians accused of stealing from whites were summarily killed. Indian accusations of miners raping women or stealing supplies were never pursued.

It came to a head when Indians in the region practiced summary justice themselves, resulting in Stevens and 30 armed men dashing into a Spokane village on Nov. 27, 1857, demanding to know immediately if the tribe was choosing peace or war.

Stevens was rattled by unrest among the Yakama and the Cayuse. The Spokane, Coeur d'Alene and bands of what are now the Colville Confederated Tribes took a few days to assemble and, in early December, listened to Stevens pitch the idea of a reservation for their own safety.

Garry, in his response, pointed out the lack of justice for the murder of Indians as key to the rage that was tilting the region towards war. Addressing injustice could prevent war, not moving Indians out of the way.

But he appeared less than sanguine. "When I heard of the war I had two hearts and have had two hearts ever since. I have two hearts and the bad heart is a little bigger than the good."

Within the year, his world collapsed. First came Lt. Col. Edward Steptoe's expedition, which was resoundingly chased away by an angry force of Coeur d'Alene, Spokane and other area Indians.

Garry lost standing in the eyes of his people by strenuously arguing that the Spokane should stay out of the fight. In the wake of the big victory, Garry looked like a coward. When Steptoe's humiliation prompted Col. George Wright's punitive expedition, Garry lost standing in the eyes of the whites, who believed — erroneously — that Garry had urged the Spokane to fight and had brothers killed in the battles with Wright.

Garry consistently argued for peace, and, according to an oral history recorded by his great-great-grandson Joseph Garry in 1961, direct accounts of family say Garry was the only son of Ilum-spokanee (and Garry's mother).

Garry had cousins, and Joseph Garry explains in his account that the words for cousin and brother are almost identical in Salish and an unskilled interpreter could get it wrong.

Wright, of course, was implacable. Unlike Steptoe, he had superior weapons, the first use of long-range rifles and minie balls, the new rifled bullet that was later used with devastating effect in the Civil War.

The tribes here were the guinea pigs for the heavy, conically shaped lead bullet that shattered bones and created terrible wounds even from great distance. The Indians, with muskets, suffered heavy losses in the battles that ran from Four Lakes near Cheney to the plains south of the city.

"I did not come to this country to ask you for peace," Wright told

Garry. The two met at a ford in the river straight south of present-day Chief Garry Park.

"Wright's answer to Garry was to bring in the weapons and bring in the women and children and 'lay them at my feet and I will dictate the terms in which I grant you peace,'" says the artist and teacher Charlene Teters, summarizing Wright's remarks.

For the next 30 years, Garry's standing kept eroding as he negotiated with a never-ending procession of different generals and treaty commissioners and politicians seeking an ever-shrinking reservation for his band.

When the Dawes Commission visited in 1881 (meeting in a tent set up west of Monroe Street), Garry was still seeking a homeland for his people north of the river from the falls to Tum Tum. He was instead urged to move to the newly created Spokane Reservation around Wellpinit.

From horseback, he is said to have looked each commissioner in the eye and told them, "My tribesmen may go, but as for me, I will die first."

❖ ❖ ❖

The Good Indian. This was Garry's country, and he was unable to win control of it, even his own 160-acre patch he had farmed for 35 years, despite doing everything whites value in "Good Indians." He prayed and was an Episcopalian. He consistently urged peace. He adopted modern farming methods and taught them to his people as well.

He got nothing for it. In 1887, the government finally negotiated an agreement with the Spokane, but it contained no homeland.

No wonder people called him querulous, says Lynn Pankonin, a historian with the Spokane Tribe. Decades of negotiating, pursuing peace and a homeland... and for what?

"I can understand his frustration at dealing with white people and dealing with government white people," she says.

The United States was willing to pay Garry's band as much as $95,000 to move to the Colville, Coeur d'Alene or Flathead (called the Jocko Reservation at the time) reservations.

Plus they would pay elderly leaders like Garry $100 a year for 10 years. He lived to see none of this.

Most importantly, Article 4 of the 1887 agreement says that any of the Indians who had been working their own land at the time of the treaty could stay there, and the government would help when it came to "perfecting title," and the tracts would be "patented to them by the United States."

Except we all know where this is headed, right?

The next year, Garry's farm was simply taken over by a settler, Howard B. Doak, who ran an aged Garry off and burned his log storehouse full of supplies.

Accounts place the farm variously at Pleasant Prairie north of the Valley or the Peone Prairie or "at the east end of Wellesley" or most often listed as somewhere east of Hillyard. But its precise location is easily found in county records.

Turns out the farm is the SW quarter of Sec. 24, Twp. 26, Range 43. In common terms it is the land — still mostly farmland 120 years later — bounded by North Orchard Prairie Road and Palmer Road on the east and west, and south from E. Orchard Road to about E. Lincoln Lane.

This 160-acre plot was recorded by Doak, according the formal handwriting of some county clerk in the 1888 "Grantee/Grantor Book," on June 21, 1888, just five minutes before closing time. A parcel information search conducted by a title company shows the farm is now split into 22 parcels.

It appears the loss of the farm was a severe blow for Garry, then in his late 70s. He was suddenly impoverished with the loss of land and goods. He and Nina survived on the scant wages their daughter Nellie earned as a laundress in town.

Kids amused themselves by rolling rocks down upon Garry's tipi, when he set up camp at various spots in Peaceful Valley and near what is now the Sunset Highway, prompting a white landowner to invite the old man to live at the more remote Indian Canyon site where he died.

❖ ❖ ❖

"He was both a good Indian and pretty much acculturated in the ways of the white man," says Joseph Garry in his oral history.

Today, there are two ways to take the term "good Indian." In his quote, we understand his great-great-grandson Joseph Garry to mean that Garry's Indian-ness was fully intact and that he would have been respected as an Indian by other Indians.

If character traits are passed down through generations, Joseph Garry himself embodies the notion of a pretty good Indian. Raised in the Lovell Valley east of Tekoa, Joseph Garry emerged as a national powerhouse among Indians fighting U.S. government attempts to terminate reservations and destroy Indian culture. Losing the land means losing economic values and identity, he said.

"Every Indian wants to go forward and make progress, but I just don't believe the Indian should be ruthlessly torn from his land and have no choice," Joseph Garry says in the oral history.

It's a strong echo of the very things Garry stood for a century earlier. Jeanne Givens, who was niece to Joseph Garry, continued the legacy of leadership herself. Her uncle was the first Indian elected to the Idaho Legislature. She may well have been the first Indian woman elected to the same body.

University of Illinois historian Frederick Hoxie in his *Encyclopedia of the North American Indian* (1996) described Joseph Garry as "The most prominent American Indian spokesman of the 1950s."

But "good Indian" can also mean one who was compliant with whites and perhaps viewed as a sellout by other Indians.

There are stories among other Spokane, not often aired with outsiders, that go in this direction.

❖ ❖ ❖

So here we are again: Who was Garry? Sherman Alexie and Charlene Teters each say they learned nothing about Garry in public schools, at Wellpinit and Spokane, which has changed now. Teters takes a nuanced view of Garry's place in history.

"It speaks to the lack of power of the people that we had incredible leaders, but the only ones written about in history and in the mainstream are the good Indians… like Sacajawea, the ones that assimilated and helped the white man colonize. Garry is our good Indian, but I don't want to diminish him as a person.

"He was a person of his time period. He was in a position to negotiate on behalf of the people who were being slaughtered and that took a lot of courage to come forward and negotiate for his people," Teters says.

"He was smart and he was assimilated," Alexie says.

Alexie, like most Indians interviewed for this story, would rather see an artwork that acknowledges the entire Native culture rather than an individual.

"My problem with a statue honoring Garry is it freezes the past," Alexie says. It becomes just another monument to a dusty historical figure — just like statues to white generals.

He likes Ric Gendron's abstract approach that contained the word "Indian." That sort of statue shows Indians are still alive, still very real, and still walking around the city that bears their name.

"I like the idea that it's all of us — and the past and present and future of us," Alexie says.

Givens would like to see a more representational statue of her great-great-great-grandfather. "I would prefer to see a depiction of the man," she says, but is open to discussion. "He was disregarded. He was forgotten. It's very heartbreaking. It's not a pretty part of history." ∎

The famed Field Museum mammoth came from a farm in Latah, Washington, in 1876.

Mammoths of the Palouse

BY JACK NISBET

First published in the *Inlander* on April 5, 2001

In the early spring of 1873, Mr. James Glover rode through the eastern reaches of Washington Territory. The forested slopes of Tekoa Mountain flanked him on one side, and the bunchgrass mounds of the Palouse Hills rolled off to the south. Following the course of a pleasant creek, he stopped to watch a native dig new shoots of balsamroot sunflower from a sunny hillside. He had seen nothing but wild country for many miles when he came upon a man building a temporary cabin out of little poles brought down from the mountains.

"He and his family were glad to see us, like all newcomers in this country who were just beginning to get little places fixed up."

This was the family of Henry Coplen, recently arrived from the Dayton area to join two older sons who had built a home in the valley the previous fall. After a stop for lunch, Mr. Glover continued north to purchase the townsite of Spokane Falls; the next summer, young Alonzo Coplen helped drive a wagon there to buy siding and flooring from Glover's new sawmill.

The valley where the Coplens were homesteading was called Latah, "place where we get food," by the Coeur d'Alene Indians, but its stream had been known as Hangman Creek since the summary execution of the Spokane leader Qualchan on its banks during the bitter conflict of 1858. Whatever feelings lingered from that incident, Henry Coplen made it a point to remain cordial with the tribe, and over the next few years native travelers often spent the night on his hearth.

The spring of 1876 was an unusually wet one for Eastern Washington, and perhaps it was the high water that drew the Coplen brothers down to a peculiar boggy piece of land near the creek where cattle sometimes got mired. Looking back, Alonzo thought it was simple curiosity that precipitated the great adventure that began there that May.

"It was a peat formation," he later recalled, "raised a little above the level of the flat, and the top shook when one walked on it." His older brother Ben described a cluster of springs, the mouth of each one puckered a few feet above the surface of the marsh.

On the afternoon in question, the brothers began to probe one of the muddy springs with a long pole. Their rod sank through the green mat of sedges and beyond, hissing down to a depth of eight feet. On one of the thrusts, it struck something hard. Their interest piqued, the brothers mucked back to the barnyard and attached a large iron hook onto the end of their probe. They plunged this new implement into the morass, grappled about, and coaxed a large object to the surface. Upon examination it turned out to be an enormous backbone, far too large for any elk, ox, or cow. Back down went the polehook, and this time an outsized shoulder blade emerged, two feet long and almost as wide. Finally they extracted a chunk of elegant, curved ivory.

❖ ❖ ❖

There was no stopping them now. Thirty-four-year-old Ben, who had worked a stint in the Colorado silver mines, outlined a plan to drain a section of the bog. Luckily, he had a crew of siblings to help: Lewis, 30; George, 20; Alonzo, 14; and Isaac, 12. Beginning on the shore of the creek, 250 feet away from their find, they set to work slicing a deep channel through the wetland.

To keep the walls of the fresh ditch from collapsing, they drove stakes along both sides, then stuffed brush tight behind them. After working their way down through the black topsoil, they shoveled through a layer of fibrous peat, then a stratum of pure white volcanic ash sixteen inches thick, then another peat layer that was speckled with woody debris.

At a depth of around 10 feet they bottomed out on a bed of gravel, and from there the brothers began trenching steadfastly toward the targeted springhole. About halfway there, they discovered "a large stone spearhead, several stone arrowheads and a small human skull" lying on the gravel layer. Just beyond these startling finds, their shovels struck an area where the sand and gravel were blackened by what Alonzo took to be ashes and carbon from a prehistoric campfire. The budding archaeologists collected the artifacts and kept digging, holding their course for the enigmatic spring.

The excavation continued through the long days of June, and when their ambitious trench finally reached the vicinity of the original discoveries, the brothers hit a mother lode of curious bones. Some of them lay in the seeping spring water, and were solidly fossilized; others were embedded in the peat, and Ben later characterized them as "soft like soap." Even though many of these crumbled to pieces when the brothers tried to move them, it wasn't long before over a hundred bones, including seven "horns," were drying in the grasses above the bog.

A visitor to the site commented that "The horns were sort of tusks, and... were worn away several inches deep at the bottom of the turn or half circle, indicating constant use by rubbing on the ground or rocks." Smaller bones included "the remains of a cave bear, hyena, extinct birds, and a sea turtle." Neighbors arrived from miles around to gawk at the humongous specimens, and at some point the brothers decided they should exhibit this wonderful menagerie around the countryside.

Ben Coplen, a widower with wild eyebrows who had lived all over the West, was by all accounts an engaging and gregarious character. He was probably the catalyst for the tour, but Lewis and a neighbor named Bill Bohard pitched in as well. The three entrepreneurs loaded one of the farm wagons with the best of their big bones, tossed a tent on top, and took off for Walla Walla.

They rattled 12 miles west to the nascent town of Rosalia, then turned toward Colfax, 30 miles further south in the heart of the Palouse. Although only a half-dozen years old, its population reached well over a hundred souls, and it already boasted a flour mill, a saw mill, two general stores, and kerosene street lights. Apparently one of the first things Ben and Lewis did when they arrived on June 26 was find a scale and enlist volunteers to help them weigh and measure the bones. The "horn" they had brought weighed 145 pounds and measured ten feet along the outside of its curve; the pelvis tipped the scales at 135, followed by a jawbone (63 pounds) and a shoulder blade (40 pounds). A single small tooth, only half the size of the ones still set in the jaw, weighed ten pounds.

At least three onlookers in Colfax that weekend were sufficiently impressed by the exhibit to fire off letters to their favorite newspapers. J.H. Kenedy, who helped to weigh the bones, postulated in Salem's *Daily Oregon Statesman* that they belonged to "animals known by antiquists as the behemoth." The correspondant to the *Walla Walla Union* reported that the pelvis had "an opening through which a man can pass by stooping somewhat." The third letter was headlined in the *Portland Oregonian* as THE CENTENNIAL MAMMOTH, connecting the great beast with the nation's upcoming anniversary. This article was penned by a recent graduate of Corvallis College named James Edmiston, who used scientific terms like "processes" and "cartilaginous surface" to describe the vertebrae and clearly delineated the narrow parallel plates that formed the molars.

But Edmiston was not all scientific jargon; after measuring the massive thickness of one mandible, he caved in to the temptation for wordplay: "This may be more jawbone than you like to take, but existing facts cannot be avoided."

❖ ❖ ❖

As news of General Custer's defeat at the Little Big Horn roared across the countryside, the Coplen's wagonload of bones crossed the swollen Snake River on the Penewawa toll ferry. From there the brothers made for Dayton, the closest town to their previous home on Pettit Creek. They certainly would have had some old friends there to show off their bones off to, and during their brief stay a photographer named William O. Matzger took pictures of the relics. Like the Colfax correspondents, Matzger had a keen interest in scientific matters, and as soon as he developed his plates he dispatched them east to Yale University via the Lewiston and Walla Walla Stage Line.

The brothers arrived in Walla Walla just in time for the Fourth of July Centennial extravaganza, which drew a crowd estimated at 3,000 to 5,000 souls for the biggest celebration in the Inland Northwest. The Brass Band played, the Glee Club sang, and at some point during the program of patriotic music and orations full of "grand and happy thoughts," a platform containing ladies and children collapsed under the weight of the watchers. By good fortune no one was injured, and the afternoon parade of Uniques and Horribles kicked off on schedule.

The assembly drew yells of laughter as it marched down Main Street led by a small monkey turning handsprings, marshaled by a man in a gorilla suit, and "gravely followed by a baby elephant." Somewhere amidst the fanfare, local photographer Leo Schumacher discovered the Coplens and their own elephantine display. Within a few days, fresh prints labeled "the biggest 'horn' ever taken" and "the biggest jawbone in the country" graced the front of his gallery. The local *Statesman Weekly* could only comment "As for the horn we do not doubt its size, but we know that there are lots of men in this country who can show more 'jaw-bone.'"

Two weeks later, back in Latah, Mr. Philip Ritz, the official U.S. Centennial Commissioner of Washington Territory, stopped by to view "the great unknown bones." He found the brothers opening up a new pit that had already yielded fossils only four feet below the surface. Two "truly wonderful" tusks looked to be nearly twelve feet long, but only one could be extracted without destroying it. They had also discovered "the head of the monster," but the skull was too rotten to move and was left in "the black, oozy mud where it was deposited ages ago."

The excavation site had apparently become a magnet for visitors, and about this same time James Edmiston of Colfax arrived for a second look at the bones. He concluded that the animals emerging from the bog belonged to the species *Elephas primigenius* — the name that the scientific community had assigned to the woolly mammoth. When handed the tooth of a younger animal, Edmiston inventively compared it to "the head of a sucker fish, the top of the head representing the root of the tooth, the mouth the surface that has been used for nipping only."

Wrapping up his letter to the *Oregonian*, he mentioned one more tantalizing find: a piece of charcoal, lifted from the gravel bed, that looked as if it had been scored by some sort of primitive tool. Amid so much excitement, Edmiston reported that "many other persons in this country remember *they* have taken out very large bones... I have no hesitancy," he concluded, "in saying here is a large field for the geologist."

Before any geologist could arrive in the field, another pair of curious locals responded to the call for exploration. William and Thomas Donahoe, Irish immigrants from Quebec, were homesteading near the town of Rosalia. In a 1930 interview, Tom Donahoe recalled that when he and Bill heard that some neighbors had dredged up the bones of a prehistoric animal, they thought of their own spring beside Pine Creek, about twenty feet deep with a clean sandy bottom. The brothers bolted sturdy hooks onto long poles and began to probe, Coplen-style. They soon hooked onto something solid beneath the sand.

For the next two days the Donahoes tugged and pulled, constructing a farmer's arsenal of levers and gantries and calling on seven able-bodied neighbors to help. But even the combined efforts of nine grown men could not raise the object. "We found that would not do, so we started to ditch it. We expect to have it ditched and the bones out in 8 days," the brothers reported in a letter to Walla Walla. When they finally extricated the treasure, it was the biggest thing anybody had ever seen, a gargantuan skull that measured 35 inches between the eyes, 50 inches between the ears, and three and a half feet from the back of the head to the front of the nose. Even though its tusks had been torn off during the extraction, the Donahoes estimated the weight of their prize as a jaw-dropping five to six hundred pounds.

So another set of brothers found themselves astonished and eager to see more. Another amazing assortment of bones piled up around a spring, including a femur as tall as a man. Another set of curious onlookers gathered around. "About the time we had most of the bones fished out," Tom remembered, "here comes a fellow with a band of sheep, headed for Montana. When he saw those bones, he just went wild, mind you. He wanted to trade those sheep, 700 of them, for a third interest in the elephant bones. He had a partner and we said he'd better wait and talk it over with him before he made a deal, but he was dead set on getting in on the fortune from the fossils. He was lucky we didn't take him up."

If the Donahoes hesitated to jump at the first offer dangled in front of them — in fact, the very next week, a Walla Walla paper reported that the price of sheep had reached its lowest level in ten years — they were not immune to the idea of commerce. Tom told a visitor that they were confident they were sitting on a bonanza, and by the end of the summer a second set of brothers began thinking of mounting a tour of their own.

❖ ❖ ❖

At around the same time that the Donahoes were hoisting the giant skull from their spring, Ben Coplen arrived back in Walla Walla to show off the most recent diggings from his Latah bog. His new display included five more tusks as well as an assortment of ribs, teeth, and vertebrae, and Ben made it clear to the local newspapers that the bone deposit appeared to be very extensive, and would certainly produce more and greater treasures.

"Our country is famous for bones if not money," crowed one editor, as widespread reports of the two incredible discoveries continued to appear in regional newspapers.

On August 12, the *Walla Walla Union* reported that Yale Professor James Dwight Dana had responded to the Dayton photographs with his opinion that brothers had unearthed "the bones of the extinct American Elephant or Mammoth." Other people had different interpretations; on the same day, the *Eugene City Guard* informed their readers that the prehistoric relics certainly belonged to a unicorn.

In mid-August, Ben Coplen orchestrated free transport for his wares on a steamboat and set off down the Columbia for Portland. Ben was not alone — Bill Bohard had bought out Lewis's share in the enterprise, and it seems possible that brother George went along as well — but whoever comprised the troupe, they billed themselves as "the Coplen Brothers." Downstream at The Dalles, the travelers found an empty storefront near Snyder's Restaurant on Main Street to display their "Antediluvian Bones." Residents of The Dalles were no strangers to such relics. Until 1874, the Reverend Thomas Condon had maintained a fossil museum in his home there, educating both locals and tourists in the wonders of what he called "the archives of the former world."

Soon after the Coplens set up shop, *The Dalles Weekly Tribune* ran a solid paragraph of now-familiar weights and measurements, adding a calculation of 20 tons as a live weight for the beast and musing about the mysteries of the fossilization process. The brothers clearly understood the mesmerizing lure of their fossils, especially to youngsters, and followed in Reverend Condon's footsteps by inviting all the Sabbath School children to view the bones for free on Saturday afternoon. Then it was off to Portland, where their exhibit drew a long review in the *Evening Standard*. When that curious reporter speculated about the roles of climatic change and early man in the extinction of prehistoric mammoths, he raised issues that are still being debated today.

The last week of September was county fair time, and the Coplens carted their relics to the Hillsboro fairgrounds. Newspaper accounts listed their "huge prehistoric bones" along with a fire-eater; an 800-pound woman; Dr. McBride, "the king of pain," a patent medicine peddler who was "here and getting rich;" and the renowned Queen's Circus of San Francisco, with his "Centennial on Wheels and his Aggregation of Transcendental Elegance." Also present was a traveling museum of "100,000 Curiosities" from Portland under the command of Colonel T.A.

Wood, a former minister who had turned to museum curation after losing his voice. Amidst all the excitement, state Senator Kelly showed up one afternoon to stoop through the pelvis of the unearthed behemoth.

From Hillsboro, the Coplens moved on to Salem, where they were joined by Thomas Condon, now a professor at the new state university in Eugene. In a lecture delivered on the evening of October 3, Professor Condon set forth his opinion that the eastern part of the Territory used to be thickly populated with these mammoths, and described how the animals might have met their death by being mired in bogs. He believed that there was not another collection to match it in the United States.

❖ ❖ ❖

The Walla Walla County Fair ran during the same week as its Hillsboro counterpart, and numbered among its exhibits the Donahoe brothers' fabulous fossil collection. Bill and Tom had rented a booth and hired a "ballyhooer" to bark in the crowds. The ponderous skull, glittering with "gold and silver quartz in profusion," provided the main attraction, but the brothers had also wired together two six-foot leg bones for full effect. One reporter calculated that the live animal "must have been two sizes larger than the Court House." When the fair was over, Tom Donahoe figured that he made about $112 for his efforts. He and his newly married brother proceeded to sell their entire lot of fossils to a man named Nathaniel Thwing for the sum of $700 — about the same price as a herd of sheep. Without wasting any time, Mr. Thwing packed the bones and booked steamboat passage to Portland.

When the great Centennial Fair opened in Salem on October 10, the Coplen and Donahoe bones were united under the same circus tent. The Coplens handled their collection personally; Nathaniel Thwing and an associate named John Hancock displayed the Donahoe specimens. Such familiar faces from the fair circuit as Wood's Museum and Montgomery Queen's Circus were on hand, and along with horse racing, needlework prizes, and agricultural machinery, "the rival bones men" garnered several notices in the fairground jottings of local papers. One visitor, identified as Dr. Davis, "the philosopher of Harrisburg," theorized in print that "the bones of the prehistoric brute found in Washington Territory... came from the moon when the continent of Africa came down after a volcanic eruption."

As the fair came to a close, the big bones men headed off in opposite directions. The Coplens moved south on a tour of the Williamette Valley, with plans to visit Albany, Harrisburg, Junction City, and Eugene City. On October 20, the *Albany Register* waxed enthusiastic: "For great curiosities don't fail to call and see the display of fossils on Broadalbin Street. You never saw anything like it." The next day, the *Eugene City Guard* announced imminent arrival of the Coplen collection.

But somewhere between Albany and Eugene City, something happened to change Ben Coplen's plans. Perhaps it was the "Webfoot" weather — it had rained almost every day since the fair ended — or perhaps he felt the need to get back home in time to vote in what was shaping up as a dead heat election between Tilden and Hayes. For whatever reason, the November 4 edition of the *Eugene City Guard* included a succinct and disappointing headline: "NOT COMING — The fossil bones announced to be shown here, have been taken to Portland where they will be boxed and laid away. The Coplen Bros. intend to then go back to Stephens county, W.T., and continue their excavations."

Two days later the *Portland Evening Standard* reported that "The mammoth fossils found by the Coplen Bros… have been leased to the Pacific University for the use of the geological classes." With brother George soon to enroll in school there, it appeared that the fossils had found a home on the quiet campus in Forest Grove, Oregon.

Ben, for his part, kept up his gentlemanly ways. As he passed through Walla Walla on his way back home, he took out an ad in the *Walla Walla Watchman* thanking the vice president of the Oregon Steam and Navigation Company "for his kindness in allowing their mammoth bones to be shipped over their line of boats, free of charge."

Mssrs. Thwing and Hancock, meanwhile, had also been on the move. On the morning of October 26, the *San Francisco Daily Call* announced the arrival of a "curious shipment" aboard the steamship *George W. Elder*. Within a few weeks, a "Mammoth Mastodon Exhibition" opened on Kearny Street. In December, a Portland paper reported that "The mammoth bones which were on exhibition in this city recently are now astounding the people of San Francisco."

But the local astonishment must have been short-lived, for up in the Palouse, Tom Donahoe heard that the agent who had taken his bones to San Francisco had sold them to pay for his hotel bill. The purchaser of those bones might have been Colonel T.A. Wood, who had recently opened a new edition of his curiosities museum a few blocks away. This venture, however, came to "adverse results," and the museum soon closed.

❖ ❖ ❖

In late summer of 1877, a young fossil collector named Charles H. Sternberg heard stories about the Palouse mammoth bones while traveling down the Columbia. Intrigued, Sternberg located the showman who had purchased the Donahoe pieces and learned that the collection was again up for sale. Sternberg alerted the famous paleontologist Edward Drinker Cope in Philadelphia, who secured the beautiful skull and other parts, boxed and ready to ship from San Francisco. Upon Cope's death in 1897, the collection passed to the American Museum of Natural History in New York City, where it still resides today.

Sternberg, tantalized by the farmers' fantastic discoveries, mounted an expedition to explore the Palouse sites himself. In February of 1878 he hired two helpers and tackled a mud spring in the headwaters of Pine Creek. Fighting water and weather, the party recovered some fine bison skulls — one with a spearpoint embedded in its crown — but no mammoth bones.

"The farmer-fossil-hunters," he lamented, "had been more fortunate."

Sternberg visited Ben Coplen's farm in Latah in March of 1878. Ben toured him through the peculiar bog down by his creek, and recounted the glorious dig of 1876. According to a letter Sternberg penned in 1903, Ben also told Sternberg that he had pulled no less than nine mammoths from the site, and had deposited them in Forest Grove. A century and a quarter later, however, Pacific University has no record of the fossils, and it is unclear how long the Coplen bones remained in their care.

In the summer of 1886, an editor for a Chicago trade magazine traveled to Latah and interviewed Ben about his excavation a decade earlier. The editor noted that a large quantity of big bones remained in the bog, and that Ben would "probably charge nothing" to assist in future digs. Notes from this interview were forwarded to Mr. Edmond Andrews, director of the Chicago Academy of Science, who after years of careful watching had recently managed to procure 700 pounds of the original Coplen mammoth bones. Over the course of that summer, preparators at the Chicago Academy sorted through the remains of four adult mammoths in an attempt to reconstruct a single whole animal. Smaller parts were upscaled to fit the largest mold; if the crew could find nothing to go by for a particular bone, they used the skeleton of an Indian elephant as a model. Unveiled that fall, the skeleton represented the only full mammoth mount in North America, and the biggest known elephant in the world.

There is no record of Benjamin Coplen ever traveling to the Academy to admire the fruit of his labors. When that same mammoth served as the centerpiece of the Washington Pavilion at Chicago's World Columbian Exposition of 1893, Ben was just beginning his term as the first mayor of the newly incorporated town of Latah. In 1907 he moved across the state line to Plummer, Idaho, taking a few of the remaining mammoth fossils along with him and leaving the rest in the family's barn. It was in Plummer that Ben passed away in 1914.

That same year, the Field Museum of Natural History in Chicago purchased Ben Coplen's mammoth skeleton from the Chicago Academy of Science and had it boxed and stored. Six year later, remounted, the Latah mammoth occupied a central place the Field's grand exhibition of fossil mammals. Ever since then, it has inspired visitors to dream of stumbling on their own cache of primordial bones. ■

Traveling from Sicily to the wilds of the Rocky Mountains,
Fr. Joseph Cataldo built a mission in the Inland Northwest.

Man on a Mission:
Fr. Joseph Cataldo

BY ROBERT CARRIKER

First published in the *Inlander* on March 17, 2011

"I jumped," recalled Father Joseph Mary Cataldo, when he heard a knock on his bedroom door one fateful evening in January of 1885. "I jumped, and that jump saved the Rocky Mountain Mission."

Against his better judgment, Cataldo was in Fiesole, Italy — far from the many, many obligations pressing for his time back in the fledgling settlement of Spokane. But two regional bishops had insisted that he travel to Italy and appeal both to the Father General of the Society of Jesus — leader of the Jesuit order — and to the Pope himself for increased support of the Catholic community in the Inland Northwest.

Dutifully, Cataldo had taken a steamer from New York to Antwerp, Belgium, in the fall of 1884. But soon, as he had feared, his visit teetered on becoming a complete waste of time. To begin with, the Jesuit curia, or Society headquarters, was temporarily in exile from Rome and had relocated to Fiesole. Then, when Cataldo reached Tuscany, he found the Father General so ill that a substitute, a Vicar General, was making decisions in his stead.

It was from this Vicar General that Cataldo learned the Society would provide no additional resources — neither men nor money — for the remote corner of the globe they called the Rocky Mountain Mission. Society finances simply could not meet such a request. Finally, when Cataldo traveled to Rome for an audience with Pope Leo XIII, he received similar negative news.

Despair grew even deeper for Cataldo after a cablegram from America arrived at the Society's villa. The message was intended for Cataldo, but, as he recalled, "my name was not spelled well," and so the missive found its way onto the desk of the Vicar General. After reading the sad message, and realizing for whom it was intended, the Vicar General personally delivered it to Cataldo in his room.

Thus the knock at his door that echoes across the region to this day.

❖ ❖ ❖

The clipped phrases of the cablegram announced that Father Louis-Marie Ruellan, Cataldo's Vice-Superior for the Rocky Mountain Province, had died of pneumonia in Spokane. It was a crushing blow because Cataldo had placed Ruellan in charge of his many plans for Spokane for the duration of his trip to Italy. Ruellan's assignments included the construction of Spokane College, the building of a church for Saint Aloysius Parish and another church to be dedicated to Our Lady of Lourdes, with yet a fourth project taking place at Saint Michael's Indian Mission near Bigelow Gulch.

Suddenly, every prospect for Spokane appeared doomed.

But the Vicar General took an interest in the drama unfolding so far away and became so distressed at the genuine sadness of the priest from Spokane that, according to Cataldo's memoirs, he undertook an impetuous action without consulting others. The Vicar "went to his room and wrote for me a letter, to all the Provincials of the Society, in which he said all he could, except ordering them … to help, each one as he could, the Missions of the Rocky Mountains."

Thus, Cataldo gained a special passport to enter European and American Jesuit schools, where he could recruit students to join the Rocky Mountain Mission, or the Catholic community in Spokane, or the college being built there.

The foundation of modern Spokane was sealed as the Vicar General wrote that letter.

Writing to a confidant, Cataldo confessed that as much as Ruellan had worked diligently for the Society in Spokane ("a hero among heroes," he anointed him) "he will be of much greater use to us in heaven than he would have been had he stayed with us here below."

Using the Vicar's letter as his entrée, Cataldo prowled Western Europe deep into the year of 1885. Then he transferred his energies to visiting seminaries across the Eastern United States. Cataldo approximated in his notes the number of priestly recruits he gathered in Europe and America at 31, but he chose not to count the Jesuit brothers, which would boost the tally to probably 50 men.

The Vicar General's call to service had turned the tide for the Rocky Mountain Mission and Spokane. Six of his recruits became future presidents of Gonzaga College, seven if you count Father John McHugh who is considered a "second generation volunteer," meaning he came to the Pacific Northwest after hearing about Cataldo's recruitment efforts from another person.

Indeed, Cataldo's jump at the knock on that door in Fiesole saved four decades of hard work by the Jesuits in the Inland Northwest and paved the way for the Society's future success in Spokane.

❖ ❖ ❖

Cataldo brought considerable experience to the job of Superior of the Rocky Mountain Mission when the Father General appointed him in 1877. Forty years old, a Sicilian by birth, Cataldo had entered the Society of Jesus at the age of 15. He began his studies in Italy and Belgium and completed them at Santa Clara College in California, where he interacted with veteran Jesuit missionaries, including Father Gregory Mengarini, a colleague of Father Peter De Smet, the initiator of Jesuit presence in the Pacific Northwest. In 1865, Cataldo volunteered for the Rocky Mountain Missions.

After his arrival in the Pacific Northwest, Cataldo lived among several tribes. He became an accomplished linguist, eventually mastering more than a dozen Native American languages. Cataldo became so involved with Indian affairs that he was, at one point in 1877, accused by a federal Indian agent of being an accomplice to Chief Joseph in the Nez Perce War.

As the Superior of the Rocky Mountain Missions from 1877 to 1893, Father Cataldo exhibited a single-minded and unreserved commitment to Native Americans. It disturbed him to see the Indian's casual commitment to Christianity. Their once legendary zeal for the Jesuit message began to diminish with the influx of gold seekers into the Pacific Northwest; their disinterest accelerated during armed conflicts over reservation lands, and it reached its nadir after the arrival of permanent settlers to the region.

Consequently, progress by the missionaries in such areas as gambling, superstition, polygamy and revenge slowed. Training the tribesmen in agriculture and animal husbandry was essential, but not sufficient by itself to withstand the destructive influence of whites. Clearly, Cataldo found, the Jesuits would have to modify the conduct of the pioneers as well as the Indians.

"If we do not attend to [the] spiritual welfare [of the whites], their bad example will so completely influence the Indians, even the Catholic Indians, that in a few years they will be entirely lost to the Church and become infidels," Cataldo wrote to his superiors.

To make the Rocky Mountain Missions more effective, Cataldo advocated reopening closed missions, establishing new ones, and upgrading old, decaying stations. Equally important, he would see to the building of reservation boarding schools. These schools would feed a "prestigious central college" for both white and Indian young men to be located in Spokane, Washington Territory. We must "insist on our schools, and show the Indians that our schools are good not only for them but also for whites," concluded Cataldo.

❖ ❖ ❖

Cataldo's words resonated with the businessmen of Spokan Falls. They knew their history, but they could also predict the future. In 1871, the Northern Pacific Railroad had announced that it was coming to Washington Territory and it would cross the Spokane River at the falls. While some pioneers relocated to the falls area and built a sawmill and stores, the community remained so isolated that in 1874 all 23 residents celebrated Christmas dinner together. A decade later, the federal census of 1880 credited the town with 350 souls.

The railroad arrived on June 25, 1881, and the excited city incorporated and even added an "e" to its name; within a year, the population of Spokane Falls grew to nearly 1,000. Still, it irritated Spokane leaders that Cheney became Spokane County's seat of government and that Pasco had the most railroad connections in the region. Spokane Falls had abundant waterpower, schools, a business community, the Post Street Bridge, a

YMCA, a city library — even a sidewalk. What Spokane Falls needed next was something the other cities did not have, something that would certify its reputation as a progressive urban environment.

Spokane needed a Jesuit college.

Father Cataldo's plans for Spokane College — Jesuit tradition at the time referred to as-yet undedicated colleges by their location — were put in motion when he purchased a half-section of land along the Spokane River in 1881 for $936. When his Jesuit superior in Rome questioned the logic of this action, Cataldo defended himself: "I acted hastily, but not impulsively." He promised 16 affluent businessmen willing to pledge money to the college that the founding faculty would include "an able teacher of physics and chemistry and someone well qualified to teach English literature."

Soon a kiln was making 350,000 bricks for campus construction, and by 1884 the outer walls of the administration building were up and the roof was on. The Spokane *Evening Review* triumphed in the progress when it wrote in the May 22, 1885, issue that the "fine brick college" was the "new ornament to our lovely town" and will "attract the many new families who have delayed their coming here on account of the absence of a Catholic church and college."

❖   ❖   ❖

Never one to stand pat, Cataldo continued to purchase land: a half-section near Bigelow Gulch for Saint Michael's Indian Mission Church, a lot in the Cannon Hill section of the city and a portion of a cemetery to be used for Catholics only.

Aegidius Junger, Bishop of Nesqually (later the Seattle Diocese), held jurisdiction over Spokane Falls at this time, and he wanted to see parishes established. Cataldo laid out his first chapel on the property he had purchased for the college. Considering that Cataldo had only two other Jesuits living with him in Spokane — Aloysius Jacquet and Aloysius Robaut — there is little mystery about the naming of the match-box sized Saint Aloysius chapel.

Jacquet and Robaut were, themselves, named for Saint Aloysius Gonzaga, the patron saint of young students. From a wealthy family in Northern Italy, Gonzaga died in 1591 at age 23, serving victims of the plague as part of his Jesuit mission in Rome. When it was time to give Spokane College a proper name, why not complete the picture? St.

Aloysius Church and Gonzaga University both honor the same saint.

Cataldo located a second church on a piece of property that he picked up from James Glover, these three lots being on the south side of the Spokane River at Main and Bernard streets. Four months later, Cataldo paid $400 for two additional lots there.

On Christmas Day in 1881, a dozen people attended Mass at Saint Joseph at Main and Bernard; meantime, at Saint Michael's Mission, some 300 Native Americans crowded into the new church.

The special assignment of Father Louis-Marie Ruellan, Cataldo's Vice-Superior for the Rocky Mountain Province, was to minister to the Catholics of Spokane Falls. In 1884 he initiated plans for a new brick church, thanks in large measure to the generosity of his family in France. Ruellan never liked the name Saint Joseph for a church, so he changed it to Our Lady of Lourdes of the Rocky Mountains. While he decided the Catholic school project could wait (until 1886), Ruellan supervised the projects at Spokane College, Saint Michael's Mission, Saint Aloysius and Our Lady of Lourdes.

Cataldo usually resided at the Coeur d'Alene Mission of the Sacred Heart, commonly referred to as Cataldo Mission, and from there he managed the activities of 54 Jesuits in a province that stretched from the Pacific Ocean to present-day Billings, Montana.

Using some of the money that Cataldo had begged in Europe during 1885 — an amount equal to $176,800 in 2010 currency — Gonzaga College opened in 1887 with an enviable teacher-to-student ratio: A faculty of 20 Jesuits welcomed 18 students in that inaugural class.

Early education was a part of the Jesuit mission, too, and that tradition remains today at Gonzaga Preparatory School — one of four Jesuit high schools in the Pacific Northwest. The student body that would ultimately be known as G-Prep was moved around, from small, basement classrooms around the campus to military barracks to, finally, its current location on Euclid Avenue. Although for many years Gonzaga High School was a department inside Gonzaga College, the two schools' history has always been intertwined. Gonzaga Prep also traces its start to 1887.

It was a busy year, as in 1887 an all-brick church for Our Lady of Lourdes was also completed. (The laying of the cornerstone for a new Our Lady of Lourdes Church at its present site on Riverside Avenue would take place on June 28, 1903; that church became a cathedral when Pope Pius X formed the Spokane Diocese on December 17, 1913.)

During the spring of 1889, most of the talk in Washington Territory centered on the prospect of statehood. Olympia, the territorial capital, was neither prosperous nor a population center and therefore seemed an unlikely choice to be the state capitol. Perhaps it should be Seattle or Ellensburg or Spokane. But then, as Congress struggled to review Washington Territory's statehood petition, the main topic of conversation changed to the subject of fire. A conflagration destroyed 30 blocks of Seattle on June 6; Ellensburg lost its downtown to a firestorm on the Fourth of July; and the Great Spokane Fire on August 4 charred 32 bocks of the business district. With many of its urban landscapes leveled, Olympia became the state capitol when Washington became a state in November 1889.

Clearly, 1890 would be a year of change for the state and for each of the recovering cities, but especially Spokane.

Father Cataldo welcomed the idea of change, for he had been proposing exactly that for the past several years. Spokane's close proximity to the silver mines of North Idaho created for the city both prosperity and a boom in population. Bishop Junger, writing from the headquarters of the Nesqually Diocese in Vancouver, Washington, insisted that the Jesuits establish new parishes in Spokane. Indeed, in 1890 the accommodating Jesuits did build a new frame church on Spokane's north side and gave it an old name, Saint Joseph.

But Cataldo could not tolerate any more expansion. He had, for some time, encouraged the bishop to at least take responsibility for Our Lady of Lourdes parish because, in addition to the care of three churches in Spokane, the Jesuits were responsible for two smaller schools and Saint Michael's Mission.

The Jesuits were too thinly spaced, Cataldo asserted, to properly manage their Indian missions. Under Cataldo, the number of Indian missions increased from nine to 15, and most of them contained self-supporting farms and herds of livestock. Some had orphanages and hospitals. By 1890, more than 1,000 Indian children were registered in Jesuit mission schools in the Pacific Northwest.

In May of 1890, the bishop and the superior met face-to-face in Spokane to resolve the situation. They agreed to divide Spokane Falls into "4 sections destined to become 4 different parishes" with the river being the division line east and west and Howard Street the line north and south. "The bishop will take charge of 3 parishes; the fourth one will be left to the Society."

Thus, "Father Cataldo, in the name of the Society, dispossessed himself in favor of the Bishop of all the different Church properties" which the Society had acquired in Spokane with the exception of the college, the chapel of Saint Aloysius and the property of Saint Ignatius Prep. Cataldo estimated that the value of the property he yielded, exclusive of the buildings, was "worth at the present moment not less than one hundred and twenty thousand dollars, so we consider that our Society (and thank God for that) makes a very handsome donation to the Diocese."

For all intents and purposes, the Jesuits left parish work in Spokane to the diocese at that moment and limited themselves to their educational mission.

❖ ❖ ❖

Released from the duties of being Superior of the Rocky Mountain Mission after 16 years, Father Cataldo launched several new careers as a missionary. It was the reason he had come to America in the first place, and he determined to end his career doing that work.

Beginning in 1893 he spent three years in eastern Montana on the Crow Indian Reservation. Then followed 14 months in Alaska, four years on the Umatilla Indian Reservation near Pendleton, Oregon, and, finally, Cataldo established a permanent home for himself among the Nez Perce Indians. The formation of schools for the tribe became his primary interest.

At the age of 70, Cataldo was assigned to a parish that preferred an Italian-speaking pastor. It was not a good fit — "We are here for the Indians," he reminded his superiors — so he was allowed to return to the Nez Perce.

In 1924, Cataldo broke his hip and leg, and while mending he discovered a new career: soliciting funds for the Indian missions. The old man, now able to hobble around only on crutches, allowed himself to be the center of a series of celebrations. There was a much-publicized pilgrimage to Cataldo Mission. Lewiston, Idaho, turned out in large numbers to celebrate Cataldo's 75 years as a Jesuit. Between March 12 and March 17, 1928, over 2,000 Spokane citizens joined Cataldo in a series of banquets and celebrations for his 92nd birthday. Twenty-four days later,

Cataldo passed away.

When asked at his birthday celebration what good advice he had been given during his long career, Cataldo replied: "I have met only one good prophet — the missionary who told me in 1865 that I might not live long elsewhere, but in the Rocky Mountain Missions, among the Indians and with a Cayuse pony beneath me, I would reach old age." ■

The destroyed concentrator in Wardner, Idaho, after the Dynamite Express made a stop.

News of the Year: 1899

BY RON MYERS

First published in the *Inlander* on March 24, 1999

TROUBLE IN THE COEUR D'ALENES

The morning of May 2, 1899, was chilly in Spokane — a dusting of snow had even covered the Palouse hills on the previous morning. But by 7 am, 75 men of Company M, 24th U.S. Infantry from Fort George Wright were called to duty in the battle between labor and management that was being waged in the Silver Valley of North Idaho. The men marched out Riverside Avenue, through Spokane's downtown, turned north on Howard, crossed the bridge and boarded a train at the Union depot, bound for Wardner, Idaho.

The morning march was no public parade; there were few citizens on the street. No cheering farewells saw the troops off. This may have been because of the relatively widespread racial bigotry of the era; all soldiers of the 24th with rank below lieutenant were black. This was the year Fort George Wright opened, and its first garrison was made up of African Americans. Although heroes for taking San Juan Hill in Cuba (an act Teddy Roosevelt was widely credited with), the 24th was never embraced by Spokane.

The event did not pass without notice, however, as the labor fight made big headlines after a mob of 1,000 union miners escalated the decade-old conflict on April 29 by dynamiting Wardner's Bunker Hill and Sullivan mines' ore concentrator "off the map," as the *Spokesman-Review* put it.

The struggle between fabulously rich mine owners and the unionized miners was a polarizing issue throughout the West, capturing all the class distinctions and economic angst of the turning century. People chose sides as their consciences dictated.

The fateful day began as any other for Levi Hutton, later to become rich off his own mining claim with his wife May. Hutton took the locomotive he operated up the tracks from Wallace to the head of Burke Canyon, where he would collect the filled ore cars for processing back down in the valley. Although he knew the labor situation was particularly touchy just then, he didn't know that the trip he was setting out upon would live on in local lore as the "Dynamite Express."

At his last stop above Burke, Hutton, who relayed his tale in the investigations that followed, was told by his conductor to pick up more box cars to take on passengers. Someone put a gun in his ribs to help him understand why.

As the train chugged down the canyon, there was a stop at the Frisco powder house near Gem to load 3,000 pounds of powder. The Dynamite Express then stopped every half-mile for more men, some masked. Finally arriving in Wallace, Hutton looked out to find 20 armed men surrounding the train. The leaders told the engineer to take her on down to Wardner on the Oregon Railway and Navigation Company tracks. Hutton argued that this was too dangerous, but one look down the barrel of a Winchester convinced him to go ahead.

The Kellogg depot was the railhead for Wardner's mines and mills. The train reached the depot just before noon. By this time nearly 1,000 men were jammed into 10 cars. The masked men — about 200 strong — were armed with Winchesters, shotguns and baseball bats. An advance party of 150 marched on down the tracks toward the Wardner mill. In their advancing spray of bullets, this group ended up killing one of its own men, one of the enemy, taking a couple prisoners and finally finding the ore concentrator — among the largest and most expensive structures of its kind on the continent — to be abandoned.

The advance crew then sent word to the main force to bring on the dynamite. To many on hand, this seemed like a replay of a similar drama from back in 1892, when union miners threatened the use of dynamite to negotiate better salaries. Perhaps only a handful knew that, this time, the dynamite was going to be put to use. Sixty 50-pound boxes of dynamite were placed at three locations beneath the concentrator. At about 2:30 in the afternoon, the fuses were lit. In a few seconds, the three blasts reduced the mill to splintered wood and billows of dust. Within minutes, everyone was back on the train for a triumphant return to Wallace, with pro-union farmers and townspeople cheering along the way.

But the story doesn't end there. As with many historical turning points, the explosion at Bunker Hill was still felt well after the concentrator was rebuilt and order was restored. J. Anthony Lukas, the late author of *Big Trouble*, which details these events, argues that the moment in the final spring of the 19th century framed the debate over the sharing of wealth in America in a way that is as pertinent today as it was then.

Just after the news of the explosion leaked out, a flurry of communiques began to travel the telegraph wires between mine owners in Portland, the governor's office in Boise and, eventually, all the way back to the White House, where a preoccupied William McKinley empowered his Secretary of War to deal with the issue. The decision that was made resulted in one of the more peculiar chapters in American history: Martial law was declared in the Silver Valley, with federal and state troops brought in to restore order.

Company M from Spokane was the first regiment of the 24th to arrive (others were en route from other forts throughout the West), and once there, the soldiers set about rounding up suspected union members or union sympathizers. It quickly became apparent that there was no way to distinguish suspects, and most men, including two of the three Shoshone County commissioners, wound up under arrest and kept in the "old bullpen," a two-story barn near Kellogg. Within a couple of days, the detainees numbered about 1,000 — the same count estimated to be involved in the Dynamite Express.

But as stories started to spread about what was happening in the Coeur d'Alenes, politicians in Washington, D.C., and prominent labor leaders in New York City began to sound the alarm that the military had declared martial law and suspended the rights of Americans under dubious circumstances. McKinley, facing reelection, lost his resolve, and bureaucrats at every level began to point fingers and cover their butts. Except one. Idaho Gov. Frank Steunenberg was the lone politician who took responsibility for taking such measures to restore order.

By July, only 150 were still detained and the 24th was preparing to ship out to the Philippines. In the end, one man, Paul Corcoran, was convicted of the dynamiting and sentenced to 20 years in prison.

The bloody post script to the story came in late 1905, when Steunenberg was killed by a bomb wired to his garden gate. That murder, the focus of *Big Trouble*, "set off a struggle for the soul of America," wrote Lukas.

Harry Orchard, who later confessed to the Steunenberg murder, said it was in retaliation for the brutal carrying out of the 1899 martial law in the Coeur d'Alenes. Orchard (who, ironically, had shared ownership with the Huttons, August Paulsen and Henry Day in the Hercules mine until he lost it in a poker game) claimed he was acting under the direction of leaders of the Western Federation of Miners like Big Bill Haywood, who later became a leader of the Industrial Workers of the World, or the Wobblies.

Orchard's final revelation? He claimed that he was the one who lit the first fuse at Bunker Hill on that fateful day.

COMMERCE AND TECHNOLOGY

To those who watched the century change, the years between 1800 and 1899 must have seemed like the greatest of all centuries for scientific invention and technology. And as the century neared its end, there was no letup in sight. Two familiar products of today, aspirin and magnetic recording tape, were both developed in 1899. And though there were fewer than 8,000 cars registered in the U.S. (and none in Spokane), the world's great automobile age was at the door — as was the age of flight, with the Wright brothers already dreaming their dreams.

And the horse was being conditioned for ultimate retirement by the bicycle — the most common form of personal transportation in 1899 (though they were a little pricey, selling for upwards of $30).

Spokane's population was estimated by the 1899 City Directory at 47,047. This estimate did not include about 10,000 transients who also made Spokane home part of the year, usually in the winter when work was scarce. This permanent population was an annual gain of around 5,000 residents, a doubling of the previous increase. And there were other measurable signs of progress. Bank deposits and clearances were each up about a third. Government receipts of the Post Office and Internal Revenue Department receipts were up as high as 35 percent. The total value of real estate transactions was nearly $9 million, and the total value of building permits was $1.2 million. Fourteen lumber mills were in operation, and Spokane was the largest flour-milling center west of the Rockies.

Also, hydroelectric power was rapidly developing in the hands of Washington Water Power. Although bad luck hit in 1899, causing the company to default on its bonds, it did successfully reorganize and continue to furnish power over long, rugged distances to the Coeur d'Alene mining district — a remarkable feat.

Making generous use of their immense, ever-growing fortunes, Spokane's tycoons threw up one castle after another for most of the decade, with Kirtland Cutter usually the architect. One of these mansions finished in 1899 was the Patrick Clark house in Browne's Addition — later Patsy Clark's restaurant.

All this prosperity at the top and flaunting of newly found wealth was fairly typical of the nation, which was experiencing good times, as years had passed since the painful recession of 1893.

THE SPORTING DISTRICT

At the end of the last century, downtown Spokane found itself in a different dilemma than it faces today: Rather than trying to stimulate activity downtown, civic leaders were actively trying to curb it. At issue was the city's "Sporting District," or "Tenderloin" — the area south of the river between Stevens and Post. In 1899, it was estimated that about 1,000 prostitutes worked the district, which was also a magnet for gambling and drinking to the Inland Northwest's miners, loggers and migrant farm workers looking for a place to spend their wages.

One of the most controversial of the lures used by the sporting ladies was a popular feature in the "variety theaters." Along the walls of the auditorium sat small rooms called boxes, with lockable doors and curtains. Reformers claimed that 97 boxes were housed in the city's 40 saloons and that 30 of them had couches which "permit immorality in the most depraved form." The girls who worked these boxes were called "box rustlers." In the words of the *Spokesman-Review*: "The moral sense of the community has been shocked by the coarse, lascivious influences exerted behind the curtains of secret boxes, where half-clad women plead with occupants to buy liquor at prices absurdly in excess of the prices charged on the main floor of the theatre."

The variety theaters and sporting houses often organized Sunday sashays down Riverside. The legitimate stars of these theaters would be in the leading carriages, but the parade also included working girls dressed up in their finest. Josey Tripp ran a busy sporting house on Post Street with more than 20 Creole girls. Tripp and a few of her favorite employees often drove around town in a fine coach drawn by a team of spirited steeds, and she was catered to by all the best shops on Riverside. Josey Tripp had a fondness for betting the horses and attracted considerable attention at the racetrack, which she often attended with her most flamboyant girls.

Carl H. Trunk, author of a collection of historical anecdotes titled *The History of the City of Spokane*, documented a more sinister business being run by K. Takahashi. Takahashi owned a big restaurant on the 500 block of West Main. Trunk claims he abused a policy of the Japanese government, which allowed Japanese in the United States to send for wives in Japan. All they needed to do was send a picture, and a woman would be sent. Takahashi leased the alley behind his restaurant and set up rooms where he sold the services of his "brides." After several years of this behavior, the government caught on to the racket and deported Takahashi.

Gambling houses were concentrated along lower Howard Street, one of the largest being the Coeur d'Alene Theatre and Gambling Hall at Front (now Spokane Falls), owned by "Dutch" Jake Goetz and Harry Baer.

A headline in the September 26, 1899, Spokane *Chronicle* read: "Shut The Town Tight … Police Ordered to Close Every Gambling Hall and House Of Ill Fame in Spokane." But it was a false alarm, since the vice businesses in town remained wide open. The business community opposed shutting down these dens of iniquity, using the argument that they brought money to town. But some who claimed to have studied the facts thought there was more to it: that married local businessmen were the major customers in the tenderloin, rather than single, itinerant workers.

The forces of virtue and sobriety waged a mostly losing battle in the final year of the 19th century. But they did not give up and occasionally won a skirmish or two. They would have to keep working for another decade to clean up the sporting district, but the heat they put on forced at least one to leave the city.

Andy Green wanted to move his roadhouse out near the new Fort Wright. The new location would place him just beyond the reach of Sheriff Cole, who had repeatedly shut him down. Neighbors didn't want the new roadhouse near them, so Green argued that the new site would better serve the new army post. But when the county commissioners called in the post's Chaplain Bateman for confirmation, they heard the following, as reported in the *Chronicle*: "This roadhouse is destructive of discipline. During one month during which it was open in this one company there occurred more than 100 cases of summary court martial, a large portion of which were due to its influence. It prompts absences without leave, insubordination, and is destructive to the morals of the garrison." Green was not granted his new license.

Another group active in separating people from their money, the medicine pitchmen, operated along Main and Front between Howard and Stevens. In an era of patent medicines that made outrageous and often bogus claims, many took their products on the road and worked out of suitcases or horse-drawn carts. But some were more successful than others and had a roof over their head. One such business was Doctor Kelly's Medical Museum on Howard. It was "for men only" and cost a dime. The museum is described in historian Jay Kalez's 1972 book, *Saga of a Western Town, Spokane*, as a "wax replica showplace that displayed a gruesome assortment of pickled human specimens as an added attraction." And then there was Doc Kevo who worked out of his open carriage on the corner of Main and Stevens. He looked like Buffalo Bill and specialized in Mexican Soap Weed.

Doctor D.R. Butler also worked indoors, above the pipe shop at Howard and Main. The sign in his window ad boldly proclaimed "Specialist for Men" — the common euphemism for the treatment of sexually transmitted diseases.

Sometime around 1899, the famous dentist Painless Parker passed through town and pulled teeth right on the street at no charge to prove his painless method. Most of these "painless" dentists would bring along a small brass band which played loud enough to drown out any yelling on the part of the patients. But this noise interfered with the other pitchmen, so dentists were usually not welcomed by the other vendors on the street.

MILITARY MIGHT

By 1898, the United States had been dabbling in the European game of imperialism for a few years and the nation was forging an empire in the process. The pivotal moment in that process was the war with Spain. Started over Cuba, and sparked by the sinking of the USS Maine, the war sprawled into the Pacific and resulted in the victorious U.S. becoming a world power with control of Guam, the Philippines, Puerto Rico and Cuba. Almost daily, the Spokane papers brought to readers news of this struggle and the growing empire. And 1899 was filled with events that brought the nation's new powerful perspective and the patriotism it stirred to Spokane's doorstep.

Perhaps most gripping was the story of Ensign John Robert Monaghan, the son of a wealthy Spokane businessman and promoter. Monaghan graduated from the Naval Academy in 1895, having been a member of Gonzaga University's very first graduating class in 1891. He then served with distinction in the Far East and Latin America until 1899, when he was rewarded with a promotion and assigned to the USS Philadelphia. In the spring of 1899, his ship was dispatched to Upola, Western Samoa, which the U.S. used as a coaling station for their steam-driven battleships during the Spanish-American War.

Since 1890, the United States had maintained a strategic interest in the islands of Western Samoa because of the coaling station. The British and Germans also had similar interests, and the three countries formed a joint protectorate. By 1899, however, the native population was rising up against the U.S. and the British (a situation perhaps prompted by the Germans).

In any case, Monaghan went ashore on April 1 as part of an advance patrol, and he was killed in an ambush by native tribesmen. He died a hero's death in that he refused to abandon a wounded comrade, leaving himself as an easy target. The balance of Monaghan's patrol party returned to find the two men's decapitated bodies. John Monaghan's story was relayed halfway around the world and told in large headlines back in Spokane. His funeral was held on June 27, and in the words of the *Spokesman-Review*, "it was a sight not to be forgotten." The entire city shut down for the funeral; the day before, 15,000 people had filed through city hall to view the hero's casket.

A statue of Ensign Monaghan was erected in 1906 were it now stands, at Riverside and Monroe.

The military mood of the time also inspired an all-out effort in the late-1890s to have a federal fort built on the banks of the Spokane River. Some city leaders pushed the post as a spur to patriotism in the community, but as usual, the expected economic benefits were what truly carried the day. The U.S. Army liked the site, and after a short battle, Congress gave approval for construction — as long as the city would donate 1,000 acres of land and guarantee water along with other infrastructure. Fort George Wright was named for one of the more vicious generals in the U.S. Army's West-taming forces of a few decades before.

Spokane residents were thrilled when the first buildings were ready to receive troops in the early part of 1899. But when soldiers arrived, Spokane suffered a "momentous shock." The crowd waiting at the train station for the first soldiers expected to see returning heroes from the Philippines. But instead, they saw more than 100 African American soldiers of Company M, 24th Infantry, arriving from Utah. Despite the fact that many of these soldiers were war heroes of the bloody Battle of Santiago and San Juan Hill in Cuba, some Spokane residents worked like mad to have the soldiers replaced. But it never happened, and the town support and interest in Fort Wright faded from the front pages (until they were dispatched to North Idaho a few months later).

The Spokane press did make an effort to change public opinion, however. When the black troops left for the Philippines in 1900, the Spokane *Chronicle* noted, "It is quite within the truth to state that the conduct of these men has been generally exemplary." And many of the black soldiers observed that prejudice existing in Southern cities was not as prevalent in Spokane — although the relations were extremely bitter between these men and the arrested Idaho miners they were sent to guard shortly after their arrival.

As the Spanish-American war came to a close in 1899, the U.S. made the decision to take possession of the Philippine Islands. The Filipino people, led by their great hero Emilio Aguinaldo, fought the takeover, first diplomatically then with arms. Aguinaldo always claimed the United States had promised him independence after the defeat of Spain — although there is no evidence to support his claim. President William McKinley claimed he was carrying out America's Manifest Destiny, saying that the United States desired the Philippines out of moral obligations of "duty and humanity."

On November 6, 1899, Spokane put on a tremendous heroes' welcome for volunteers and regulars returning from service in the Philippines. The train dropped the soldiers off in the morning "amid the shrieking of whistles, the ringing of bells and cheers from thousands of human throats." Within an hour, a grand parade began to form on Riverside and the side streets.

The rest of the parade was formed of boys from the public schools and Gonzaga College. Each school displayed a banner with a patriotic slogan, including this prescient message: "The Schoolboys of Today Will Take Care of Uncle Sam in the Future." ∎

May Hutton (front left) at her mining camp kitchen prior to striking it rich.

Winning the Vote:
May Arkwright Hutton

BY EMALEE GRUSS GILLIS

First published in the *Inlander* on March 6, 2008

The scene would have made May Hutton proud: Senator Hillary Clinton, the first woman with a legitimate chance to become her party's presidential nominee, standing onstage in a packed auditorium at Spokane's West Central Community Center, explaining to people why they should elect her the nation's next chief executive. Many of those watching were women, eager to cast their votes to make the senator the first of her gender to lead the most powerful nation on earth.

Today, Clinton and others can look back on a long history of accomplishments by women in politics. Those accomplishments were made possible by the groundwork laid by women like May Arkwright Hutton, whose efforts led to the successful vote in 1910 to extend to women in Washington state the right to vote.

Hutton was a leader of the women's suffrage movement in Eastern Washington. In addition to her many other accomplishments, she was one of the first two women to attend a national convention for the Democratic Party.

Given Hutton's strong political interest, she certainly would have thrown herself into the middle of this year's hotly contested nomination process. She would have toiled for her favorite candidate, made arguments for that candidate at her neighborhood caucus, perhaps even become a delegate at her party's national convention this summer. Knowing that she was from the second most populous western state, she would have understood why Washington would be critical as each candidate worked to win support in the West.

A century ago Hutton wanted for Washington women what their counterparts in Idaho had already had for a decade, although she had no illusions about what that would mean. She said in one of her many speeches, "When I ask the voters of Washington to trust their women as Idaho has done … I bring to you no record of marvelous results accomplished by Idaho women since their enfranchisement."

Hutton didn't give a flowery account of the glories gained by women's enfranchisement in her neighboring state. Instead, she argued that there must be great change in the political arena before women outgrew "the swaddling clothes of their newly acquired citizenship."

❖ ❖ ❖

The roots of May Hutton's activism go back to her early childhood. She was born in Ohio in 1860. Before the age of 10, she lost her mother. When she was in the third grade, her father asked her to quit school to tend to her blind grandfather. Living in poverty, she cooked and cleaned for him and led him by the hand wherever he wanted to go. Because he couldn't see, her grandfather loved to hear all he could. Hutton would lead him to the village square where he listened for hours to political speeches or to the words of evangelists. Hutton listened, too. She was introduced to a variety of issues, including those surrounding the mistreatment of miners.

Hutton came from an economically impoverished home, but the environment in which she lived was intellectually very rich. In addition to the words in the square, Hutton was exposed to the talk of political men who visited at the family home. Those men included William McKinley, who was a family friend long before he became president in 1897. One evening, after she served him cider and doughnuts, McKinley told her that when she reached womanhood he hoped for "an enlightened age of equal suffrage." Her father responded that he would rather she find a good husband.

Later in her life, Hutton duplicated that rich environment filled with intellectuals in her own home, hosting U.S. Senator William Borah, libertarian Clarence Darrow and poet and author Ella Wheeler Wilcox.

Hutton was a risk taker. At the age of 23, she sought her fortune by leaving Ohio and heading to Idaho with 40 miners. She worked hard as a saloon cook in the mining areas of the Idaho Panhandle, then bought her own boarding house. In 1887, she married one of her customers, locomotive engineer Levi Hutton (the same Levi Hutton who eventually built the Hutton Building in Spokane and started the Hutton Settlement, a home for children). May Hutton cooked her own wedding dinner for 50 guests.

In 1897, the Huttons invested $550 with five others in the Hercules Mine in Idaho. For four years they toiled long hours at the mine with no success. After working in the kitchen, Hutton was known to put on overalls, unheard of in her Victorian time, and work alongside the men down in the mine. Then, in 1901, one of their partners struck a rich vein of ore. They had found silver. The Huttons became millionaires overnight.

Soon the couple had luxuries that they'd never had before. One of May Hutton's luxuries was time. She was freed from her long daily work to pursue her passions. She began to educate herself, including a study of Shakespeare. Through her wide reading, she became exceptionally well-informed on the issues of the day.

Her strong attraction to the challenges of the working class and her connections to the unions pushed her to run for Idaho office in 1904. Women in Idaho had already gained suffrage. Hutton was defeated by only 80 votes. To explain the loss, she pointed to the mine owners who contributed $20,000 to her opponent's campaign.

Levi and May Hutton moved to Spokane in 1906 for a variety of reasons including increased business possibilities for Levi. By moving to the state of Washington, May Hutton not only lost the right to become a candidate, she lost her right to vote. She immediately devoted herself to the suffrage cause.

❖ ❖ ❖

The woman's right to vote in the state of Washington was a long, hard-fought battle filled with advances and disappointing setbacks. In 1883, the territorial government of Washington passed legislation that gave women the vote, only to have the courts declare the new law unconstitutional in 1884. That cycle of win and loss was repeated. In 1888, the Legislature approved "An Act to Enfranchise Women," which was voided later that same year by the Territorial Supreme Court. It took more than 20 years of fighting after that court decision before enfranchisement successfully passed the legislature and became permanent.

Spokane society was not used to a lusty woman like the 6-foot-tall, 225-pound Hutton, who dressed outlandishly and spoke her mind forcefully and directly. While other women wore subdued Victorian dress, Hutton wore bright colors, flowered prints and wide-brimmed hats with roses spilling down to her shoulders.

Not only did Hutton frequently rub the women of Spokane the wrong way, she often was in conflict with other suffrage leaders in Washington. After Hutton returned from a Seattle suffrage convention where her views were not endorsed, she formed her own organization based in Spokane: the Washington Political Equality League.

Between 1906 and 1910, during the heyday of Hutton's activism around suffrage, she clipped hundreds of articles and pasted them into ledger books that she used as scrapbooks. Hutton's pasted pages, now housed at the Northwest Museum of Arts and Culture, include articles that quote directly from her speeches as well as other long-yellowed articles reflecting her broad interests. The material opens a window into May Hutton's life and provides insight into the fascinating history of her time.

In the early 1900s Hutton fought against many anti-suffrage attacks from both women and men. A woman identified in one of the clipped articles from Hutton's scrapbooks simply as "Mrs. Bacon" argued for "more babies, not more ballots." Bacon said, "No woman living will ever do a great work who could not have borne great children, and if she can bear great children she can do no other great work." Bacon admonished women "not to paint pictures or to attempt to make laws, but to make men."

Hutton responded, "According to this acknowledgement, Mrs. Bacon's writing cannot be very great, and how great her children will be time will tell." Hutton goes on to write that, although motherhood is beautiful, economic conditions have forced women out of the home "to earn her bread, and have made motherhood a burden instead of a joy as God intended it to be."

Hutton also had a rebuff for another argument with the slogan "No Babies, No Ballots." A priest, Father Phelan of St. Louis, suggested that only men and women with babies should be allowed to vote. Archbishop Diomede Falconia, apostolic delegate to the United States, heartily agreed with the St. Louis clergyman.

One suffragist, D. A. Steward, condemned th notion vigorously, saying, "It's simply preposterous!" Another suffragist, W. J. Gleason, stated, "What have babies to do with ballots?" She argued that a widowed woman with property should have the same right to vote in the country that she supports as any man. Hutton simply commented that if only men and women with babies were allowed both Father Phelan and Archbishop Falconia would be disqualified from voting, along with all priests and bishops.

Sometimes the accusations made about suffragists and their roles in the family hit a tender spot. Hutton said, "The charge is made that suffragists don't care for the home. I can only say that suffragists do. In our family, while we have no children of our own, yet we have raised five girls. And now the grandchildren are coming around to the house. Then people charge that I am in suffrage work because I haven't the mother instinct."

In other cases, Hutton strongly defended the ability of suffragists to contribute to the home environment. For example, a woman named F. F. Emery joked that there should be a cooking school for the husbands of suffragists. Hutton responded that there should be cooking schools for all men, not just those who were husbands of suffragists. She went on to suggest that the courses be taught by some of the most well-known suffragists because, "among them are some of the best cooks in Spokane."

Hutton often talked about the benefits of suffrage to homemakers. "It is a good thing for woman to have the ballot. The more a woman knows about civil government the better homemaker she will be. Management of a household these days is an economic problem. A woman should know why prices are as high as they are and why wages are as low as they are. The wife cannot make ends meet now."

The articles that fill May Hutton's scrapbooks are without notation or marks, with one exception. One article she clipped attacked the intelligence of women. Hutton underlined with a heavily pressed black pen this quote from Professor Frederick Starr, a famous scientist and ethnological explorer from the University of Chicago: "Women are not civilized. Furthermore, they should not be civilized. What's more, they can't be for the fundamental nature of woman is barbaric, and it is better so ..."

In a related clipped article, Reverend J. E. Seth stated, "It is an open question whether women will vote as intelligently as man. If she does not vote more intelligently than men, then nothing is gained by women suffrage, either for its country or its people." He added, "Politics must have its very deepest roots in the home and in the home atmosphere. Therefore, let us be careful lest we drag woman down from her high station to equal that of man."

Even the president of a major university at the time argued against women's suffrage. In one article in Hutton's scrapbooks, W. E. Stone, the president of Purdue University is quoted as saying, "I am not in favor of extending the voting privilege to women. ... I do not think that women are less intelligent than men or less well qualified to exercise suffrage than a good many men who now do so, but I think that the sphere of work and influence of women is not directly concerned with politics or business affairs in general. I am not convinced that any considerable number of women wishes for suffrage and I see no reason at this time why it should be granted."

Although Hutton did not respond directly to these articles, in another she said, "I think self-supporting, self-respecting women of the present age resent the implied thought that man is woman's superior. Man is not and has never been woman's superior — only in brute strength."

Some clippings are amusing. One says, "Let the women have the ballot, that will relieve the men of half the work and worry of running the government. Besides it will put all men in a Garden of Eden where they can blame the women for all the political blunders that are made."

Women, even strong women like May Hutton, became discouraged at times. But they kept fighting. For example, Hutton said, "I believe that the injustice of denying the woman the ballot is so glaring and the justice of the cause so apparent that it will soon rouse the women from the apathy into which they have fallen."

❖ ❖ ❖

On November 8, 1910, the suffragists' hard work finally paid off as women's enfranchisement passed in the general election in the state of Washington and became law. Hutton must have been deeply satisfied to paste in her scrapbook, "Resolved; that the National American Woman's Suffrage Association, in Convention assembled, send greeting to the men of Washington in appreciation of the twenty-four thousand majority vote, which gave their women the ballot, and whose example must be, and has already been, an inspiration to men of other States."

Hutton also received a letter of congratulations from Governor M.

E. Hay on November 11, 1910. The Governor said, "The quiet, ladylike manner in which this campaign was conducted has won the admiration of all our people and won success at the polls." This letter must have amused Hutton given that "quiet" was not a word typically used to describe her.

Hutton gave credit to one group in particular in winning the vote for women in Washington and in the other four states where women were enfranchised. In a letter, she states, "The enfranchised women of the five free States of this Republic owe this privilege principally to organized labor."

After that successful campaign, Hutton stayed involved in women's political issues. She helped establish mining unions and worked throughout her life for the underprivileged. She also brought property under her own name for the sole purpose of being qualified to serve on a jury and became one of the first two women to serve on a Spokane County jury.

In one clipped article Hutton said, "I am often asked the question of what women are going to do with the ballot now that they have it." She pointed with pride to work by enfranchised Seattle women that resulted in ousting political grafters. She also pointed with equal pride to Spokane women who helped inaugurate a commission form of government and helped elect a set of new commissioners. She commented, "I invariably reply that I hope, trust and believe that women will use the ballot as intelligent, enlightened human beings would use any weapon placed in their hands whereby they could better the conditions under which humanity lives."

In addition to continuing work on women's issues in Washington, Hutton supported the cause of the vote in other states. On her way home from the national Democratic Party convention in Baltimore in 1912, Hutton made 13 political speeches in Ohio. She was reported to be "the saddest woman in Spokane when she read that news of the defeat of the woman's suffrage amendment in Ohio." To encourage Hutton, Elizabeth Hauser from Ohio's suffrage movement wrote a letter to her stating, "It cannot be defeated. It is doomed to success."

Indeed, the suffrage movement won its ultimate victory in 1919 and 1920 — after May Hutton's death — when three-fourths of the U.S. states ratified the 19th Amendment to the Constitution, bringing the vote to the women in every state.

Hutton did not always concur with the ways of the suffrage movement in other countries. She was particularly opposed to militant approaches in England at the time. When British suffragist Emmeline Goulden Pankhurst wired Hutton and said she would give a dozen speeches in the state of Washington for $1,200, Hutton wired back and said she would give Pankhurst $1,200 to stay away.

Whether she agreed with their methods or not, Hutton followed suffrage movements from afar. She clipped articles from places like France and Germany. One article said, "The recent elections have demonstrated that the suffragette movement in France is not yet in the realm of practical politics."

An article from Chicago describes suffragists handing out yellow cards saying, "No Vote, No Tax," to women standing in line for a special tax assessment. The article notes that some women left their place in line after receiving the cards.

At the national level, Hutton had a strong dislike for President Theodore Roosevelt and wrote articles against him. Her negative feelings for him started when he said, "Only twice should a woman's name appear in public, when she marries and when she dies."

Hutton's public work diminished after 1912 as her health deteriorated. She died in 1915 at the age of 55. People of all classes and backgrounds attended her Spokane funeral.

Now, nearly a century after Washington women received the franchise, our state is represented by women at the highest levels, including Gov. Chris Gregoire, and two U.S. senators, Patty Murray and Maria Cantwell. Hillary Clinton's candidacy has proven that millions of Americans will vote for a woman for president. Perhaps if Hutton were still with us, she would address women in politics today with the words she sometimes used to close her letters: "Yours in liberty, May Arkwright Hutton." ∎

Ensign John Robert Monaghan was killed in Samoa in 1899.

Strange Days at Monaghan Mansion

BY PATRICK HEALD

First published in the *Inlander* on Oct. 26, 1994

E xactly 20 years ago, a series of unexplained events began at
Gonzaga University's Music Building, formerly the Monaghan
Mansion. These events, typical haunted house fare, were so
pronounced that a Catholic priest decided to conduct a series of blessings
on the building — a move that was widely reported as an old fashioned,
Roman Catholic exorcism.

Today, the priest who conducted the blessings would rather not talk
about the incidents that took place between September 1974 and February
1975. And although the building certainly looks the part, no one has ever
been able to point to a specific reason the Monaghan Mansion would be
haunted.

❖ ❖ ❖

It all started when Fr. Walter Leedale, an associate professor of music,
began to get reports from students that they had heard mysterious footsteps
in the music building in September of 1974. Skeptically, Leedale began
sleeping in his office in the building to quiet the rumors. But rather than
silence the rumors, Leedale began to believe what students had been telling
him. His first eye-opening experience was when he was going to open a
locked door. As he directed the key to the lock, the door opened in front of

him. Inside, the room was empty.

One evening in January, Leedale distinctly heard a flute being played from within the building. But upon searching the building, he found neither flute nor flutist.

He remembered the tune, however, and one day while playing it on the piano, the building's housekeeper overheard him. She told Leedale that the tune was the same as one she heard one evening in November. She told Leedale that one Friday evening she returned to the building to pick up something she forgot and heard someone playing the organ. The front door to the building was uncharacteristically unlocked, but the organ room was locked. She retrieved the key, opened the door and found the organ running but the room otherwise empty. The windows were all locked.

On another evening, when Leedale and a security officer were in the basement, they heard growling noises from behind a locked door. The men decided it was the wind, but when Leedale returned later and opened the door, he found that wind could not have been the culprit. He also found a cello with all its strings broken and an axe buried in a chopping block that was normally stored outside the sealed room.

But the event that captured the most attention took place the evening of Feb. 24, when Leedale, Daniel Brenner (the music department chairman), a student and two security guards say they had a physical brush with the other-worldly. While chatting outside the building, a guard noticed something in a third-floor window. Then both guards saw a similarly wispy figure in a second-floor window. Leedale was in his office on the ground floor at the time and nothing could be found anywhere else in the building. When the group made it up to the third floor to investigate, Leedale said something made his skin crawl when they were in a narrow hallway. One guard reported a strangling sensation. And Brenner said that he had trouble moving forward.

The next day, Leedale began blessing the building. He read exorcism prayers in the house six times over four days. On several occasions, Leedale and Brenner told reporters later, the crucifix that Leedale was wearing around his neck would sway, even though there was no breeze inside the building. Leedale had to eventually clasp the half-pound cross while he said the prayers.

After the six blessings, Leedale said that the strange occurrences ended and the music building was back to normal.

Shortly after this series of incidents and the blessings, word leaked out that an exorcism had been conducted at Gonzaga University. After all, *The Exorcist* was in movie theaters just two years before, and the subject of the rarely used Roman Catholic sacrament was a public fascination more than ever. Leedale was subjected to a fair amount of publicity and, after telling his side of the story to the media to clear the air, quit talking about the whole episode. For the record, the university has said that the sacrament of exorcism is designed to be used on a person, not a house. Prayers of blessing like the ones Leedale used are common in the Roman Catholic faith for the blessing of new homes. University officials never appreciated the publicity generated by the event, and even today they downplay it.

The *Spokesman-Review* ran a story on the incident on April 13, 1975. In it, the reporter found lots of skepticism among other faculty members and former students. In a story in the Gonzaga *Bulletin*, one of the security guards even said he didn't have the trouble the others did on the third floor that evening because he never read *The Exorcist*. And someone later admitted to moving the axe and wood block into the locked room in the basement.

In the 20 years since it all happened, the story has taken on a life of its own on the campus of the private school. But through all the speculation, no one has ever made a solid case for why the building would be haunted. There was a suicide in 1973 that was widely believed to have happened in the building, but it actually happened in another building on campus.

So perhaps we must look further back, into the history of the house that has stood at the corner of Boone and Lidgerwood since 1898. And yes, you will find a tragic story, a story that gives the Monaghan Mansion the credentials you'd expect of any haunted house.

❖ ❖ ❖

In 1858, at the tender age of 19 and just two years off the boat from Ireland, James Monaghan became a Columbia River ferryman during the great westward migration. He ran supplies from Colville to Bridgeport, where pioneers boarded riverboats to finish their journeys to the Willamette Valley. In fact, a set of rapids near the Nespelem River still bears his name. Monaghan later became the storemaster at the Spokane trading post, and in 1886 moved his family into Spokane proper. Over the years, Monaghan held interests in gold mines, banks and railroads, and he's regarded as one of the founding fathers of Spokane.

In 1898, three years after his wife and the mother of his six children died, Monaghan commissioned the construction of a mansion of stone. If ever a house looked the part of a residence for spirits, Monaghan's brooding castle fits the bill. James Monaghan died Jan. 13, 1916. He outlived his eldest son, John Robert Monaghan, by nearly 17 years.

And it is John Robert Monaghan who met with the sort of untimely death that ghost stories are made of. Born in Chewelah in 1873, John Robert was a member of the very first class at Gonzaga University and was the first Washington state resident to graduate from the Naval Academy. In 1899, he was assigned to the U.S.S. Philadelphia. When trouble erupted in Samoa, the Philadelphia was sent there. Two rival chieftains were making war, and ships from the U.S., England and Germany were anchored in the harbor to make peace. After two weeks of bombarding the island to little effect, the English and American captains sent a contingent ashore to ferret out the elusive natives. Naturally, they walked directly into the jaws of a trap.

Natives descended upon the foreigners, who were armed with just one automatic gun that jammed. An American, Lt. Philip Lansdale, was wounded so badly in the leg that he couldn't retreat with the others. John Robert Monaghan stayed back in an attempt to save his comrade, and both were killed. The next day, when a landing party retrieved the bodies, they found that both had been beheaded.

Monaghan's body was returned to the U.S., and the funeral that followed was one of the largest that Spokane had ever seen. But when the casket was placed inside the Monaghan Mansion, photographs show it was decorated with upside-down crosses — just strange enough to feed the stories surrounding the mansion. Is John Robert Monaghan haunting the family home?

You can see John Robert Monaghan today at the corner of Riverside and Monroe, just in front of the Spokane Club. The statue commemorating his valor was unveiled in October of 1906.

Gonzaga University began to lease the Monaghan home in 1939, and purchased it in 1942 for $10,000. It has housed the music program ever since. There are no known reports of strange occurrences prior to the mid-1970s.

Despite Leedale's claims that all the trouble ended on Feb. 28, 1975, there have been recent reports that keep the mystery of the Monaghan Mansion alive.

❖ ❖ ❖

Al Vogel, a campus security officer in 1979, told Doug Clark of the *Spokesman-Review* that during that year he had an experience in the Music Building that left him to wonder. He used to find the doors to the building unlocked one minute and locked the next, and he would see lights mysteriously flicker on and off.

One evening, after seeing some dancing lights, Vogel and his partner went in to investigate. There was some shuffling of feet — human feet as it turned out. In a basement room they found three students with flashlights looking sheepish. It turns out, all the uproar over the exorcism brought a lot of thrillseekers to the building, which explained the doors and the lights.

Stepped up security has eliminated the problem. But that same evening, after running off the intruders, Vogel and the other man decided to check the building one more time. Up on the third-floor, after hearing a noise, Vogel turned, expecting to see his partner but instead found a chalkboard rolling up next to him. His partner was way across the room.

When the two men tried to push the chalkboard, it barely moved at all.

Now jump ahead to the present day. Amy Harper, a sophomore at GU, works at Monaghan Hall. She says she isn't aware of all the history surrounding the building, but her story seems to fit the legend.

On a recent Monday night at about 10 pm, up on that infamous third floor, Harper was putting a television and stereo into a room at the end of the narrow hall. As she returned, passing by a set of tables leaned up against the wall, she saw a shadow pass behind her. She turned around in time to see the tables tip all the way over — not slide to the ground — and hit the wall on the other side of the hall. She said she wasn't sure if she brushed them or if something else caused them to fall over. Either way, she got a little scare that night.

❖ ❖ ❖

"Honest to God, I don't know what it was," said Fr. Leedale, recalling his experience in that very same hallway for the *Review* in 1975. "But I can say that Christians believe there are evil forces in the world, and that we, as Christians, pray to God to protect us from them, or for the strength to deal with them. This is what I was doing at the music building." ■

The Moscow tombstone of Winnifred Booth.

Mystery of the Moscow Flowers

BY SHERI BOGGS

First published in the *Inlander* on May 25, 2000

Cemeteries are odd places — monuments to our own mortality and strangely soothing at the same time. The grass and trees are hypnotic in their thick, green silence, and elegant markers urge visitors closer for a better look. Anyone who's ever wandered around an old cemetery knows what it's like to come across a headstone that doesn't seem quite right. Sometimes it's a row of small headstones, a grim reminder that frequent infant mortalities were once part of hardscrabble life on the Western frontier, or perhaps an epitaph that seems weirdly personal, a line from a hymn or a quote. Still, it's as if a perfectly kept lawn heals all manner of tears spilled and secrets carried to the grave.

A handful of people who have become the stuff of local legend are buried in one such cemetery on the outskirts of Moscow, Idaho. And yet, this same handful of people could have remained forgotten forever if not for the work of Mary Reed, a historian for the Latah County Historical Society. Reed had just moved to the area 20 years ago when she took on her first project — a reissue of the long-out-of-print novel *Buffalo Coat* by Carol Ryrie Brink.

"I discovered that the woman who wrote *Buffalo Coat* had also written *Caddie Woodlawn*, which was one of my favorite childhood books," says Reed. "I was just astonished that this woman had grown up in Moscow, the book [*Buffalo Coat*] was set in Moscow, and she was a very famous writer, but no one talked about her."

It's ironic that the townspeople had almost forgotten about Brink, as *Buffalo Coat*, her first adult novel, was inspired by both the tragic events that had shaped the tiny town of Moscow at the turn of the 20th century and the gossip that flourished surrounding those events. The bare facts are that three doctors — Dr. William W. Watkins (Brink's own grandfather), Dr. F. J. Ledbrooke and Dr. C.D. Parsons — who occupied the same tiny office in downtown Moscow each met an untimely end, in 1901, 1902 and 1903, respectively. Brink, who was six years old at the time of her grandfather's death, was at an impressionable age and listened, spellbound, as the adults discussed the murder of her grandfather and the scandal of Dr. Ledbrooke's suicide.

"She explained to me that she was a quiet child, and that adults would kind of forget that she was there," says Reed, who flew down to San Diego to meet Brink in 1981, a month before the author died at the age of 86. "So they would talk about things in front of her that they probably wouldn't discuss openly in front of a child. It was the climate of those times, where a lot of entertainment was talking, gossiping, really."

Dr. Watkins was one of the town's early founders who worked tirelessly to improve the tiny mountain community. In addition to his thriving medical practice and position on a number of committees, he is also credited with establishing the University of Idaho in Moscow.

"It seemed to me that she was writing about an era that was often overlooked. People are caught up in the idea of the frontier, the old wild West kind of thing," Reed continues. "But she was writing about a time — I call it the town-building period — during which these people weren't the hardy pioneers making candles, but they were the people that were building libraries and schools and establishing solid lives here."

Still, Moscow was not immune from the violence and trouble to be found in other small towns along the frontier. Dr. Watkins was killed while on his rounds in August of 1901, shot by William Steffens, a certifiably insane man who lived on the edge of town in a ramshackle old farmhouse. Apparently Watkins had scolded Steffens for mistreating his frail, elderly mother (who lived with him at the farmhouse). Steffens then went on a shooting rampage based on a list of townspeople, which included Watkins, whom he felt had wronged him in some manner. The town's sheriff was also killed by Steffens, who was later shot by a posse of townspeople after a siege lasting several hours.

Dr. Watkins' practice was taken over by an Englishman, Dr. F. J. Ledbrooke, who had just come West with his wife Alice. During the course of his short practice, he treated a young local woman named Winnifred Booth, a student at the college and the daughter of the local Methodist minister.

Less than a year after Watkins' murder, in May of 1902, Dr. Ledbrooke and Winnifred Booth were found dead together, victims of a double suicide by morphine injection, in a hotel room in nearby Orofino. The town was horrified, not only by the tragedy, but by the fact that it had occurred right under their noses. Front porch gossip became the stuff of newspaper reports, with headlines like "Miss Winnie Booth Was Hypnotized," and the assertion: "Physician and daughter of a Moscow minister go to another town, attend church, and then commit suicide."

While the headlines seem almost funny in their high-pitched Victorian melodrama by today's standards, Brink absorbed all of it, both the gossip and what little truth could be gleaned from it. When the third doctor, Dr. C.D. Parsons fell from his pack mule in the mountains and died from head injuries in 1903, the Moscow community said that the office was "hoodooed," and no one would go near it.

❖ ❖ ❖

The rumors surrounding the unlikely chain of events would most likely have faded away to nothing had they not been stashed away in the memories of a girl who was determined to become a writer. One of Brink's first novels, *Caddie Woodlawn*, was based on the pioneer girlhood of her grandmother, Caroline Woodhouse Watkins, Dr. Watkins' widow. The book won the 1936 Newbery Medal, the highest honor in children's literature, and remains as popular with modern readers as Laura Ingalls Wilder's *Little House* books. Part of the reason for the book's popularity lies with Brink's approachable, lively voice.

"At that time, there were a lot of very pretentious books for kids written by adults who wanted to teach them lessons," says Reed. "I think that's one of the reasons why *Caddie Woodlawn* is still so popular with young readers. She was able to really speak to children. In a lot of ways, that book is really amazing."

While Brink continued to write books for children, she also started working on her first novel for adults. Her original idea was to write the story of the doctor's office and what happened to the three doctors who practiced there, but she soon learned that rigorous adherence to the facts wasn't necessarily great fiction. Her publisher, Macmillan, returned the book with the statement that while the material was interesting, she had killed off the most interesting character (her grandfather, who appears as Doc Hawkins in the novel) too early in the story.

A writing seminar with Sinclair Lewis several years later inspired Brink to dust off her earlier manuscript and work it into a much more engaging form. In a letter to an aspiring young writer in 1973, Brink writes, "A couple of years later I sat in on a writing seminar given by Sinclair Lewis at the University of Minnesota. Mr. Lewis was good enough to read my first attempt, and the advice he gave me was to 'forget that this really happened, start all over again and make a good story of it.' This was good advice and I have used it ever since."

Brink took the liberty of dovetailing the events, setting up the characters of Doc Hawkins (her grandfather) and Dr. Allerton (Dr. Ledbrooke) as professional rivals, although they had never met in real life. She also had a chance to set the record straight on what she believed to be a doomed love affair. In *Buffalo Coat*, Dr. Allerton falls in love with young Jenny Walden (Winnifred Booth), almost against his will, and Brink successfully navigates the precarious development of their growing affection for one another, setting up for the reader the fatal outcome of their relationship. It was a significant departure from news accounts of the day, as well as a rejection of popular opinion at the time.

"The newspaper reports were that he had hypnotized her, because who wanted to believe that this could happen?" says Reed. "You had to find an excuse, a reason for this to happen, and you're not going to say that a minister's daughter would commit adultery with a married man. So I think it must have been something like this: People needed to believe that she was an innocent victim. And there was already mistrust of him, because he was an outsider."

Still, some of the town's old-timers, many of whom were interviewed for the Latah County Historical Society's oral history archives, recalled Ledbrooke as having supernatural powers. "We don't have a lot of people talking about it. But of the people who really did talk about this was one of our great county storytellers, Lola Clyde. She was a very articulate and passionate person," says Reed, adding with a chuckle, "I imagine that her telling the story this way probably convinced a lot of people."

In Brink's version, what emerges is an honorable, bittersweet and surprisingly believable romance. Brink skirts the physical possibilities of the relationship in favor of the developing respect and love between her two tragic characters.

"The important thing about that affair was not the sex part of it but the dilemma these people were in," says Reed. "There weren't too many options at the time." Both Ledbrooke and Booth came from deeply religious backgrounds and lived in a community where divorce was unthinkable. It's also important to remember the mores of the time, when living in sin was a serious matter, not a lighthearted joke.

As Brink writes in the introduction to the 1980 edition of *Buffalo Coat*: "These were two very religious people who believed that, because he was married, loving each other was a sin. A divorce would have ruined his career and her reputation and would have wounded innocent victims. Yet they felt that they couldn't live without each other. Today there would have been various more-or-less easy solutions. In 1902, they saw no alternative but double suicide."

❖   ❖   ❖

Reed, who has read all the newspaper accounts in addition to Brink's novel, agrees that the suicide was a voluntary act and not an act of malevolence between perpetrator and victim.

"Winnifred was living away from home and teaching school, so she was fairly mature," Reed points out. "It's hard to say for sure, of course, neither of them left a diary or letters, but I suspect that there was an attraction on both sides."

When the novel was published in 1944, it unleashed a flood of speculation.

"Carol Brink said the telephones were ringing all over town, with people trying to figure out who it was in the book," says Reed, who adds that Brink had not lived in Moscow for some time. "It created quite a stir. It surprised Carol Brink that there was so much fuss over it. She thought everyone had forgotten her."

In addition to the gossip spreading over the small town like a prairie wildfire, the novel also kindled a small town urban legend of sorts. Since 1944, flowers have mysteriously appeared on Winnifred's grave every year on Memorial Day.

"Going out to the cemetery and seeing her grave is a very moving experience. It's all by itself at the end of a row," says Reed. "It's just this simple little headstone that has that verse carved in it that she had asked, 'There's not a friend like the lowly Jesus, no not one.'

In the suicide note that she and Ledbrooke left, they wanted to be buried together, which, of course, didn't happen. Her family must have left Moscow because none of her family is buried nearby.

From Winnifred's grave, looking north and a little to the west, Ledbrooke's headstone can be seen — it, too, resting in apparent solitude. Just a few rows back are the graves of Dr. Watkins and Caroline Woodhouse Watkins.

❖ ❖ ❖

Buffalo Coat was a remarkable success, even appearing on *The New York Times* bestseller list for several weeks in 1944 before giving way to the much more sensational *Forever Amber* and a wartime paper shortage, which limited print runs. Brink was so heartened by her success, she published two more Idaho novels, *Snow in the River* and *Strangers in the Forest*, both popular with local readers in spite of changing times in the publishing world.

"By the time she wrote *Snow in the River,* she was a little out of date," admits Mary Reed, a historian for the Latah County Historical Society. "People wanted more titillation then, and people weren't reading her books as much."

Reed's involvement has restored Brink to her rightful position as one of Idaho's foremost literary writers. "It kind of became a mission for me to make Idahoans aware of a native author," says Reed, who notes that while Ezra Pound lived in Idaho briefly as a child, and Ernest Hemingway spent the last years of his life there, it was rare to find an author of national stature who had written *about* Idaho. "It seemed to me that here was a woman who not only wrote about Idaho but lived here, so she was what I would call a *real* Idaho writer."

Part of Reed's work has involved educating the community about Brink, who overcame significant difficulties of her own. In addition to losing her grandfather, Brink's father died when she was four, and her mother committed suicide three years and a day after the death of Brink's grandfather. She was raised by her grandmother, whose character Anna in *Buffalo Coat* gives the novel both its open moral vision and an appreciation for the beauty and unpredictability of life on the frontier.

"She was someone who really overcame a lot of personal tragedies, but she was determined to live a productive life and be cheerful about things," says Reed of Brink. "She said once, 'I was a lonely child but not an unhappy one.'"

If anything, Brink's past gave her an uncanny ability to understand the harsh realities and unexpected joys of life in a small mountain town. Her three Idaho books, which were republished in 1993 along with her memoir *A Chain of Hands* by WSU Press, are still popular with local history buffs, readers of regional literature and folks who just plain enjoy a good story. And in spite of changing trends in contemporary literature, many readers find her work is still relevant.

Brink's legacy is quietly memorialized around town, from the English Department building on the U of I campus named in her honor, to the children's wing in the Carnegie Library in Moscow, to even a rustic little park on Paradise Creek dedicated to her. ∎

Photographer Charles Libby in 1930 with some of his work — all available for purchase.

EASTERN WASHINGTON STATE HISTORICAL SOCIETY PHOTO

The Viewfinder: Charles Libby

BY LISA WAANANEN JONES

First published in the *Inlander* on July 18, 2013

C harles A. Libby hauled his camera down the steep stairs on the north side of the river and stood on a wooden platform at the base of the lower falls. The young man turned his lens south toward the steel lattice of the Monroe Street Bridge and the silhouette of the downtown skyline, but his eye was on the water.

What did Libby see in the falls? Did he see the graceful dancing of the spray, the sun off the water, the water tossed into droplets of light before crashing on the wet, black rocks below? Did he see it in black and white, as it would emerge later from the darkroom chemicals? Was he thinking of people who might want to purchase such an image, or was he just thinking of shadow and light?

He took a frame, and another. He took a whole series, each one a slightly different moment isolated from the roar of the ever-crashing falls.

❖ ❖ ❖

Imagine Spokane as it was a century ago: A bustling city rebuilt after the devastating 1889 fire, flush with insurance money and mining fortunes, the downtown streets busy with streetcars and automobiles beneath a tangle of wires. If you can picture those streets, or elegant social gatherings at the Davenport Hotel, or the Grand Coulee Dam under construction, you most likely have seen Libby's work. Our memories are made of Libby's photographs.

Many other photographers made their homes in Spokane in the early days and the decades that followed, but no other photographer took so many photos over so many years. By the time he retired in 1962, Libby had witnessed and recorded more than six decades of construction sites, businesses, social gatherings and special occasions. He photographed four Presidents and every landmark of the region, and left more than 200,000 negatives. Local historians have described his photographs and meticulous ledger books as a "monumental collection" and an "invaluable historical resource." Libby left a vast and valuable record of Spokane's growth — but very little of himself.

Libby arrived in Spokane in 1898 at age 19. His family — mother, older brother and two sisters — moved from Olympia after the death of his father, a mining engineer who had came out to the West Coast from Maine. Unlike Olympia, Spokane was booming. The population had doubled in the 10 years since the fire.

Libby helped his older sister Addie in the photography studio she opened in downtown Spokane. By 1902 the pair split off to operate their own studios. The reason isn't clear — it may have been a business choice, or more likely a difference of vision.

Photography was not uncommon at that time — Spokane had eight photographers listed in the 1900 city directory — but most photographers stayed in the studio and specialized in portraits. Most who traveled specialized in landscapes and stereoscopes. The equipment was bulky and heavy; controlling the light was essential. Libby took portraits throughout his career, but made a name for his studio by taking his camera out of it. His sister's advertisement in 1903 said: "Visit the Libby Art Studio for Artistic Photographs." Libby called himself a "commercial fotografer," and he would come to you.

He married Gretchen Schlussler in 1905. Their only child, Charles A. Libby Jr., was born two years later. On Sundays the Libbys would pack a picnic and take a ride on the streetcar, and if a building under construction or grand new home caught Libby's eye, he would stop to photograph it, just in case someone might want a print.

❖ ❖ ❖

Libby was a hustler. He must have been tireless. Decades later, his son recalled reluctantly working weekends as a boy out at Liberty Lake and Coeur d'Alene, where companies and clubs would hold huge picnics. The Libbys would take a group photo, drive back to the studio in Spokane to develop a proof, then rush back to the gathering hoping to catch everyone before they left. The proofs would be passed around, and anyone who wanted a copy would write a name and address on the back.

In those days the Libbys used Kodak's Cirkut panoramic camera, and they'd get the whole party to pause from their picnic and line up in long rows for a photo. Every group had a joker, the younger Libby later recalled, who would stand at one end as the camera started and then run around back so he'd show up on both ends of the photo. Many times a photo was ruined with blurry faces as everyone else turned to look at what was going on behind them.

Libby was an innovator; both he and his son were fascinated by technology and machines. It was a time when, if a family bought a new car or a company bought a new fleet, the Libbys would get a call to come photograph the proud occasion. The Libbys showed up for the wrecks, too — they took thousands of photos of derailed trains and crashed cars for insurance companies.

Around the same time the Libbys photographed the National Air Races at Felts Field in 1927, the younger Libby took photography to the sky with some of the region's first aerial shots. He would go up with pilots he knew at Felts Field and step out onto the wing with an arm wrapped around a strut and both hands on the camera. A local company made a special harness that tied him to the plane in case he lost his balance.

❖ ❖ ❖

Beginning in 1933, the Libbys were hired to photograph the full construction of the Grand Coulee Dam. From the excavation to many years afterward, the Libbys took their equipment to the site and the surrounding hills to photograph the piles of earth and gravel, the concrete and steel, the heavy trucks and cranes reshaping the landscape.

In 1934, President Franklin Delano Roosevelt came to visit the dam, and was driven to a promontory on the east side of the Columbia River to view the site before addressing the crowd. Unlike the Associated Press photographers swarming for the president's visit, Libby knew his way around and waited patiently beside a rock. As the car rolled by, he snapped an up-close photograph of FDR's face — shadowed by the wide brim of his hat — that became one of his most widely seen.

For the younger Libby, photography was always a business. It was a profession, often technologically interesting, but he claimed no love of photography as an art. "Maybe this sounds kind of cold-hearted," he said in an interview after he'd retired, "but to me it was a dollars-and-cents proposition. That's all."

His fondest words, though, were for the days spent in the sun at the Grand Coulee Dam site.

"I remember all day long down at the dam taking pictures of the excavation and driving the steel and the pouring of the concrete," he said. "I think that's when I enjoyed photography the most."

❖ ❖ ❖

Charles Libby Sr. died in 1966 at age 86, four years after he retired. In 1969 his son sold the business to Keith Henry, who had previously worked for the company, and it was Henry who recognized the value and immensity of the studio's collection. It wasn't a collection he could maintain himself, and he made arrangements with the Eastern Washington State Historical Society to sell a portion of the negatives and donate the rest in 1987.

By the time a portion of the collection was preserved and discussed in 1979, it was necessary for historians to point out that Libby photographs do not show a complete record of Spokane's past. Libby and his son took very few photos of Spokane's black and Asian communities; they did not photograph crime or poverty.

While photographers working for the Farm Security Administration captured migrant families and Dust Bowl landscapes during the Great Depression, Libby photographed ladies in furs crowded around the window displays at Sears, Roebuck and Company. While war photographers wired home images of fallen G.I.s in World War II, Libby photographed department stores and soda fountains. While early documentary photographers captured the tenement slums and child workers at the turn of the century, Libby photographed the falls.

"They didn't go out and take pictures of slums unless someone hired them to take pictures of slums, and no one did," the Washington State

Historical Society's curator of special collections, Edward Nolan, said at the time of an exhibit in 1991.

There's a modern impulse to apologize, to justify — to clear Libby of culpability by vacating his intent. It was all a matter of business: He aimed his lens in the direction that money asked him to.

What happened to the young man who stood beside the crashing falls, watching the spray and the light? Maybe that was idle practice; maybe he no longer had time, with a family to care for and a business to run. He stopped riding the streetcar looking for grand houses; he bought a car and rushed to keep up with requests. Through his decades of ledgers, we know who Libby worked for on which days, when he had his cameras cleaned and what price he paid for his darkroom chemicals.

The photos of Libby himself show a man at ease, with a broad smile and dark-rimmed glasses. Even in portraits he carries a look of eager momentum, like he is used to being on the move. As a young man he jokes around in the studio; as a grandfather, he sits to the side of a sofa and makes faces at the baby to get her to smile.

His work was driven by money, surely, but Libby was not merely a businessman or a technician. He was not an impassive recorder of his clients' wishes. It's clear in the casual pride of men standing beside trucks with their hands in pockets and hat brims obscuring their eyes; in the light falling through the trees onto children dressed in white at Natatorium Park; in the symmetry of pyramids of canned goods and polished floors, the repetition of shining factory assembly lines, the dark curve of rails bending to meet the horizon — he was biased toward beauty in lines and light, and presented his subjects the way they imagined themselves.

Libby was an optimist. He sold the idea that special occasions require evidence, and he predicted our nostalgia.

Over the years, Libby appears in some of his own photos as a shadow in the lower corner of the frame. It's not clear whether this was simply accidental, unavoidable given the position of the sun, or if it was something more intentional. Did he want us to take notice? Was he deliberately leaving evidence of himself?

A newspaper article printed in 1949, when the company opened a new state-of-the-art studio on Lincoln Street between Second and Third, described Libby as a "clear-eyed, robust-looking man." He was 70 years old, and he'd been photographing Spokane for more than half a century. He and his son had decided to build after their longtime studio in the

Exchange Building was torn down.

"The wrecking crews have had to chase me out of most of the offices I ever had," Libby said.

None of the buildings where he worked still stand. Not the first one, on the second floor of a narrow building on Post Street, nor the second, in the old Granite Building that stood where the Paulsen Building is now. The studio on Lincoln that was new in 1949 was torn down less than three decades later. Libby admired progress, and he also understood the inevitability of loss.

It's not clear what Libby wanted us to see in the shadows of himself, but they look now like blind spots, negative space — reminders of how much we might never have seen if Libby had not taken the photo, and how much of Spokane's past we see through his eyes. ■

Bernhardt Schade (straddling the barrel) with his team of German beermen.

The Brewmaster: Bernhardt Schade

BY MIKE CORRIGAN

First published in the *Inlander* on December 7, 1994

We in the Pacific Northwest have always been a thirsty lot. At the time this territory was being settled, no one was more welcome to a new community than a German immigrant with his copper brewkettle and dreams of producing the finest beer available anywhere. Oregon and Washington were opening up, bursting with untapped potential. The miners, farmers and loggers who were striving to make something of it all were, in the process, working up one hell of a thirst. And the local brewer was more than happy to supply the refreshments.

Put heavy emphasis on the word *local*. This was before Prohibition, at a time when refrigeration was a cutting-edge technology and the most popular way of keeping things cold was to put 'em on ice. Most brewers couldn't afford to ship their beer all over the country, so each region (and in most cases, each town) had its own local brewing industry to fulfill the needs of the community. It was a nice arrangement, and the variety of beers across this country must have been a wonderful thing. Everyone was happy. Well, apparently not everyone. More on the dreaded "P" word later.

The Northwest was attractive to would-be brewers not only because of the great demand for their sudsy product, but also because of the abundance of quality brewing water. Spokane was no exception. Over the years, Spokane has been home to more than a dozen breweries, most of them now long gone. Excellent local microbreweries have revived the tradition, but the glory days and the grand old breweries have been all but forgotten — most of the clues to their existence eradicated by the wheels of progress.

There was the enormous Spokane Brewing and Malting Co. on the current site of the YWCA on Broadway. Inland Brewing stretched over an entire block of Second Avenue, between Cedar and Walnut. And standing somewhat aloof, on the corner of Front Street (now Trent Avenue) and Sheridan, the B. Schade Brewing Company. Perhaps because of its location — removed from the central hub of the city — Schade's monument to fermentation has consistently eluded the wrecking ball and stands to this day as a reminder of one man's vision and dedication to a brewing tradition.

❖ ❖ ❖

Bernhardt Schade came to Spokane in 1892 to assume the position of brewmaster at Rudolph Gorkow's New York Brewery. A German immigrant, Schade had learned the art and science of beer-making during his apprenticeship at a brewery in Macon, Georgia. For 10 years he satisfied Spokane residents with "New York Beer" and himself with dreams of bigger and better things.

Including independence. By 1901, nearly every brewery in Spokane (including the New York Brewery) was either owned or operated by the Galland family of Spokane Brewing and Malting. Schade believed the time was right to break the monopoly. He left his position in 1902, and the B. Schade Brewing Company began to take shape.

His plans unfolded quietly. Then, as the brickwork for the building was to begin, the brewmaster revealed his intentions. The *Spokesman-Review* of the day bristled: "START BIG NEW BREWERY — Larger Capacity Than Any Plant Now Operating — Not In The Brewers' Combine!"

The word was out. Schade, as an independent brewer, was planning nothing less than to out-produce the local giant, Spokane Brewing. He realized what he was in for. "Of course, we will have a fight on our hands for awhile," he said, "but we count on that."

Reputed to have been designed as an exact replica of an ancient German brewery, Schade's brewing plant was an elegant example of form following function. In the stately five-story tower, malted barley, hops, yeast and water were brought together to mingle and ferment. Other areas contained the bottling works, malt house and the lagering cellars. Take a walk by the old brewery today and you can imagine what a source of local pride the structure must have been when newly constructed, with the large circular window atop the tower filled with blue-stained glass, forming the name of the proud, young brewmaster. The folks at the B. Schade Brewing Co. were, as they said, ready for a fight. And to be sure, the competition was fierce. But the family brewery prospered and was soon expanded.

❖ ❖ ❖

By 1912, the rail lines were being extended from downtown Spokane eastward. As they moved out along Front Ave., the Milwaukee Railroad encountered a small obstruction — the B. Schade Brewing Co. The road attempted to purchase the land, but Schade's asking price of nearly $1 million was a bit more than the people at Milwaukee were willing to spend for the right of way. Instead, the railroad tunneled under the brewery, an act that Bernhardt Schade regarded as nothing less than trespassing.

He sued the railroad and was ultimately awarded the sum of $65,000 in damages. He didn't stop the railroad (bottles must have rattled a bit whenever a train would run under the brewery), and the railroad didn't stop Bernhardt Schade. The truth is, the railroads didn't have to — the United States government was working on it.

Bernhardt Schade took beer making seriously. To the Schade family, beer was not only a commodity but an integral part of everyday life. It must have been difficult for him to have foreseen, even with the temperance movement gaining momentum, that not only his livelihood but part of his cultural heritage would soon be taken from him.

Whatever you want to call it, Prohibition — the "Noble Experiment" or the "damned 18th Amendment" — national prohibition of the manufacture, sale and transportation of intoxicating liquors was by any accounting a complete failure. Impossible to enforce, it served only to turn otherwise upstanding citizens against the law and made criminals into millionaires. It also served to drive many an honest, hard-working businessman into bankruptcy and despair.

Washington and Oregon had the dubious honor of leading the rest of the nation into Prohibition, going dry a full four years before the implementation of the 18th Amendment to the Constitution. On

December 31, 1915, Spokane undoubtedly experienced a New Year's Eve unlike any other.

The next morning, Schade was unemployed, forced by taw to close the doors of his beautiful Bavarian brewery forever. Three years later, the banks closed in, and in 1921, at age 51, with failing health, Bernhardt Schade took his own life.

❖ ❖ ❖

There is a story connected with the demise of the B. Schade Brewing Co. that puts a positive spin on the otherwise melancholy tale. Apparently, Schade was acquainted with a woman who had been recently widowed. The brewmaster entrusted his beer recipe to her, and she, in turn, produced enough Schade "home brew" to support herself and her family through the toughest years of the Depression. Spokane residents continued to enjoy Schade beer, albeit illicitly, in spite of Prohibition. The widow owed a large part of her success to the fact that many of her best customers had good, steady jobs at City Hall and in the police department.

Meanwhile, the brewery building was being used as shelter for transients and down-and-outers. Known by the locals as the Hotel De Gink, the shelter was set up and run by the residents themselves, with help later from the city and local businessmen.

With the repeal of Prohibition in 1933, it was inevitable that some enterprising individual would capitalize on the fact that the Schade building was built for one reason: to make copious amounts of sweet beer. It didn't take very long.

The decision of Golden Age Breweries to reopen the plant was greeted with much enthusiasm. Promising to employ upwards of 150 men and women, the new brewery would not only produce beer for thirsty, Prohibition-weary residents, it would also mean a big shot in the arm for the local economy.

The building was steam-cleaned and refitted with the latest brewing gear. The water flowed, yeast cultures were given all they could eat and the place smelled like a brewery again.

But as the memory of Prohibition faded from the minds of the general populace, a new "brewing reality" began to take shape — one that had less to do with beer-making tradition than it did with economics.

By the end of Prohibition, what was left of the brewing industry in this country began to consolidate. Large breweries, able to weather the dry years by producing nonalcoholic food products, emerged in 1933 and hit the ground running. They bought up struggling and bankrupt independent breweries and began to mass market beer varieties that would appeal to the most people. With this strategy and superior distribution networks, the large breweries increasingly made it impossible for small, local outfits to compete.

In 1948, Golden Age was sold to Bohemian Breweries (a division of Atlantic Brewing Co. of Chicago) as an addition to Bohemian's main operations at the Inland Brewing plant on Second Ave. "Bohemian Club Beer" was brewed in the Schade building until 1957, at which time beer making in the structure was discontinued for, quite possibly, the last time.

After Bohemian pulled out, the building was purchased by Inland Metals, which utilized the beautiful landmark as a storage shed for scrap metals.

In 1977, a demolition contractor with plans for a restoration became master of the estate. The restoration never materialized and the structure only fell deeper into ruin.

❖ ❖ ❖

Current owners Louis and Gailya Bonzon purchased the brewery in 1991, and in so doing may well have rescued the historic building from the ravages of time and more than three decades of neglect.

The Bonzons operate two businesses out of the old brewery, a retail carpet and flooring outlet in the back of the building and an antique mall up front. They have restored most of the main level and have plans for the renovation of the rest of the structure as well.

One possible scenario calls for the transformation of each tower floor into its own separate residential apartment. But before humans can move in, the brewery tower's current tenants need to be evicted.

"First thing we'll need to do," sighs Gailya Bonzon, "is to get rid of those pigeons,"

The pigeons are, in fact, everywhere. On a guided tour of the brewery interior, I find myself nearly jumping out of my skin as groups of the feathered beasts spring into action at my every step. Gailya seems calm, totally unfazed. I feel like we're invading their turf. But we press on.

The rooms on the upper floors are as fascinating as they are creepy. Everywhere, there are ghostly reminders of the building's glory days.

Over dark, empty doorways, the labels remain: "HOP ROOM," "LAGERING CELLAR B." In what appears to have been the tasting room, the Golden Age "shield" logo (including the phrase "God Bless America") occupies most of one wall. Several of the rooms still contain huge steel brewing vessels, too large to have been removed and sold as scrap. Every room has secrets and a story to tell.

And despite its somewhat ramshackle appearance, the building is structurally sound, having been built to stand for centuries. The Bonzons are working slowly and methodically, as time and the availability of funds permit.

More important than the renovations they've completed are the strides the Bonzons have made securing historic landmark status for the old brewery, They've managed to have it placed on a local registry and are in the process of taking it even farther.

With National Historic Landmark registration comes the grant money needed to complete the restoration that the structure so desperately needs and deserves.

But beyond that, is it possible that one day some entrepreneur might recognize the positive power of the old brewery's ghosts and decide to start a small brewing venture within these hallowed halls?

As she was closing up the antique mall one evening, I suggested this scenario to Gailya. Apparently, there has been some interest in such a plan, though nothing serious has developed as yet.

Still, we both thought it was great idea.

And I'm sure old Bernhardt Schade would agree. ∎

Nell Shipman with her pet bear, Brownie, at her Priest Lake movie studio.

Priest Lake Producer: Nell Shipman

BY TONY AND SUZANNE BAMONTE

First published in the *Inlander* on August 24, 2000

When Helen Barham was a little girl living in Victoria, B.C., she began to receive compliments on her physical attractiveness. Even as an adolescent, she was tall, self-confident and possessed an eye-catching appeal. One day, during a discussion with her mother, Helen mentioned these compliments. She asked her mother if they were right. Was it a fact that she was beautiful? Her mother responded, "Yes, you are quite pretty, but remember you did not do this yourself. It's up to you to make your insides as pretty as God has made your outside."

Helen would later become Nell Shipman, Canada's first silent screen actress. She would pioneer women's roles in screenwriting, acting and directing both in Canada and the United States. Greatly influenced by her mother's convictions and kindness, she championed the cause of humane treatment of animals used in motion pictures, essentially becoming the first animal rights activist in the United States.

Shipman's concern for the welfare of animal actors began early in her acting career. During the filming of a wildlife-related movie, Shipman observed a bobcat being shocked by electricity to make it hop and snarl and then immediately doped to make it lie still; the animal died. Another inhumane practice involved a procedure to simulate a horse being shot and crashing. Piano wire was fastened to the horse's front leg and anchored. As the horse ran from the anchor, the yards of slack wire became taut at the desired location, causing the horse to fall. Oftentimes the stunt left the horse so severely injured it had to be killed.

Shipman loved acting, especially when animals were involved. She soon vowed that somehow she would acquire her own wild animal cast and make actors of them without the use of cruelty. Though short lived, she managed to carry out her dream in the Inland Northwest. Spokane, Spokane County, Pend Oreille County and North Idaho became her stage. A glance at the Inland Northwest's early history of entertainment, including the era of silent movies, provides the stage for viewing the life and times of Nell Shipman.

❖ ❖ ❖

Shipman's parents, Arnold and Rose Barham, moved to Victoria from England. Much of their ancestry was connected either to the church, law, medicine or the Royal Navy, and the Barhams' upbringing had been influenced by their somewhat stuffy upper-middle-class Victorian standards. To this proper English couple, their second child, daughter Helen, who was a free and willful spirit, embodied the antithesis of a proper English lady.

Nell Shipman came into the world on October 25, 1892 in Victoria, B.C. Situated on Vancouver Island's southeastern tip overlooking the Strait of Juan de Fuca with the Olympic Mountains in the distance, Victoria is one of the most beautiful and oldest cities in the province of British Columbia. Its origins stem from the old Hudson's Bay Company's fort, erected there in 1843. The city was laid out in 1851 and incorporated in 1862. At the time of her birth, this little city of approximately 20,000 inhabitants was the port of call for all the Trans-Pacific steamship lines to the Orient and Australia. Its industries included salmon canneries, lumbering, iron foundries and numerous other manufacturing industries. The city and surrounding countryside was sprinkled with attractive buildings and residences.

Ten days after Shipman was born, a doctor pronounced her dead. Rushing from the cottage where she lived with her husband and four-year-old son Maurice, the grief-stricken Rose Barham carried her baby to the cliff above the straits overlooking the serenity of the mountains and water. She began rocking the dead baby in her arms. Suddenly, the baby came to life again.

Seventy-six years later, Nell Shipman wrote of this event and her nature in her autobiography:

Was there a dark-skinned bit of wild elf skittering among the sweet broom, born on the wayward sea-breeze, looking anxiously for a dwelling? A house-haunting Haunt? A soul in limbo hanging between the Devil and the Deep? Did it catch, with its hawk's eye, the little, still, white-skinned Englander and manage to nip inside, quicker than a wink? Would that account for the paradox of a Mr. and Mrs. Arnold Foster-Barham birthing, sustaining and bringing up a creature foreign to them as a Siwash, a being made of fire and water and gutter-muck, a half-wild, ornery, often vulgar, and brave-beyond-reason child who would forego convention, dodge proper education, refuse to be a lady and become, instead, not only an actress at age thirteen, but a free-wheeling, swinging, do-it-yourself-er, at home where the living is primitive and grossly lacking in human comforts? Arnold and Rose, facing the future with this thing they'd spawned, might well wonder.

At the age of six, Shipman's parents took her to see her first play, the *Boston Lilliputians*. It was cast with child actors who sang and danced. The juvenile stars of this play were Daphne and Snub Pollard. Little Helen was totally enamored by Daphne as she sang "Please Go 'Way and Let Me Sleep." From that point on, she regularly performed for whatever audiences she could capture, often imitating Daphne. Her grandfather was her best audience. She loved the attention and now wanted to become a movie actress. (Interestingly, when Shipman gave birth to twins in 1926, she named her son Charles and her daughter Daphne.)

Shipman's musical talent was discovered after the family moved to Seattle around 1899. She took lessons from Mrs. Louise Beck who had a studio in the same building that housed Frank Egan's drama school. During a recital at Mrs. Beck's studio, Shipman sat down to a grand piano and played a Chopin nocturne "far better than might be expected, almost prodigy promise." This was her first recital with adult students. At the end, she was presented with a bouquet of American Beauty roses accompanied by generous applause. Shipman's stage presence was outstanding. The thrill of it all was overwhelming to her.

Pressure and opportunity soon surrounded Nell. She had the potential for a great musical career. Her mother became an encouraging part of her daughter's ambitions, and a wealthy aunt offered to provide that opportunity. However, at the age of 13, Shipman forsook that possibility to become an actress.

❖ ❖ ❖

In 1906, she left home and joined a one-night-stand traveling road show company. The star of the show and his wife promised to protect, guide and chaperone her. At the end of that same year, Shipman wrote home from Wallace, Idaho, saying, "At last I am a Professional Actress." In reality, those times in her young life were hard and laced with many uncertainties. Still, she continued to learn and, even more importantly, became somewhat polished. The road show company soon led to other interesting acting jobs and experiences — both vaudeville and theatrical.

At the time of Shipman's rise to fame in silent movies, popular movie stars embodied two distinct female body types. The first was the physique of Venus de Milo, the famous Roman statue of the nude goddess of love. This body type had been popular since the 17th century and had become a standard of excellence for the female form. In 1916 the *Spokane Press* held a "Perfect Girl" contest in Spokane. The winner would be the woman who most closely matched the following purported measurements of the Venus statue. (Mrs. L. M. Lewis of 1427 W. Boone won this contest.)

The second idealized female figure was the Ziegfeld Follies' type. In 1920, Spokane took part of a nationwide "Salesgirls' Beauty Contest" sponsored by Florenz Ziegfeld Jr., producer of the Ziegfeld Follies. From the contest it was evident that Ziegfeld favored full-figured women, easily confirmed by examination of early Ziegfeld Follies' photos.

Nell Shipman's figure was somewhere in between the Venus de Milo and the Ziegfeld type, tending to lean more towards the latter. Her robust physical appearance conveyed a picture of health, strength and athletic ability. Shipman, in fact, was an excellent all-around athlete, especially excelling in swimming. Even as a teenager, she was considered physically beautiful. She was tall (close to six feet), had long dark brown hair, large brown eyes with an almost perfect symmetry to her face. Her physical attractiveness, with the desired "look" for the movie screen, was accompanied by growing her proficiency as an actress and pianist.

❖ ❖ ❖

At the age of 18, she met Ernest "Ernie" Shipman, manager of the Stock Company for George Baker, who owned a chain of theaters on the West

Coast. Ernie, a fast-talking womanizer, was also a marrying sort of man. Nell soon became his fourth wife. After marrying Ernest Shipman, upon his advice she changed her name from Helen to Nell, officially becoming Nell Shipman. In 1912 Shipman gave birth to her first child, a son she named Berry. While she was pregnant and unable to act, she began writing screenplays, an endeavor that would become a lifelong pursuit.

In November 1918, Shipman was offered an exclusive contract with the well-respected and creative American writer of outdoor adventure stories, James Oliver Curwood, who agreed to star Shipman in his future films. In return, she agreed to appear exclusively in Curwood productions, with Ernie Shipman as the company manager in charge of financing. This agreement resulted in the formation of the Shipman-Curwood Producing Company. Prior to this, from 1915 to 1918, Shipman had played leading roles in a dozen feature films. Two of these were based on novels by Curwood and produced by Vitagraph, which was one of the leading studios of the time. Curwood was attracted to Shipman because of her physique, courage and ability to stand up to the rigors of his outdoor films. Curwood was also obsessed with her superb head of hair, a definite asset for heroines of the day.

The first and only film this company produced was originally titled *Wapi, the Walrus*, but upon completion, the title was changed to *Back to God's Country*. It was based on a short story written by Curwood and filmed at locations in both Canada and the United States. In 1919 this film was completed at a cost of $67,000.

Because part of this production was filmed in Alberta, Canada claims Nell Shipman as its first woman filmmaker and has a commemorative postage stamp in her honor. Interestingly, one of the scenes involved Shipman swimming nude at Lesser Slave Lake in Alberta. Her pet bear, Brownie, accompanied her. Unknown to Shipman's character, she was being observed by a lecherous old fool in the midst of forming evil thoughts, when Brownie saved her from a "fate worst than death."

Shipman's nude scene was the first to be produced on the silent screen up to that time. Three years prior, Annette Kellerman played a nude scene in *A Daughter of the Gods*, but she wore a tight pink body suit. Shipman was scheduled to wear the same type of body suit. However, it kept bunching up and looked so unnatural she decided to perform the scene truly naked.

Although *Back to God's Country* was an enormous success, grossing millions, Shipman saw little of it. In 1920 she separated from Curwood and decided to form her own movie production company. Partnering with her former manager Bert Van Tuyle, she formed Nell Shipman Productions. During the first year of her new enterprise, they produced four successful short films. Their fifth film, called *The Girl from God's Country*, was a major production, but exceeded its budget and the final 12 reels was five more than the backers had requested. When both Shipman and Van Tuyle refused to cut the film, the backers canceled Shipman's contract, seized the film and reduced it to seven reels. Infuriated by this action, Shipman and Van Tuyle responded with a number of bad decisions, which essentially resulted in them and the film being somewhat blackballed. The film was released in September of 1921, but failed miserably at the box office.

During Shipman's earlier vaudeville and theater days, she had visited the Inland Northwest on many occasions and was familiar with the area's beauty and pristine wilderness. It was perfect for the type of movies she produced. Shipman contacted Wellington Playter, the actor who played the lecherous old fool in *Back to God's Country*. Playter was now living in Spokane and had a lease on the former Washington Motion Picture Corporation's studio at Minnehaha Park.

By 1920, Spokane already had a movie studio — a shuttered one. That's because before Shipman discovered the potential of Spokane and the Inland Northwest as a place to make movies, another silent film star had already come — and gone.

On Aug. 19, 1917, Tyrone Power Sr. arrived at Spokane's Great Northern Depot to great fanfare. The first Miss Spokane, Marguerite Motie, and representatives of the Spokane Ad Club, greeted him. He was honored with a dinner in the Marie Antoinette Room of the Davenport Hotel.

Following a six-day survey of Spokane's scenic possibilities, Power made the decision to establish a movie studio in Spokane. The site he picked, Minnehaha Park, was owned by the city and under the control of the Spokane Park Board. Members of the Park Board were eager for the chance to attract a movie studio to the Spokane area and quickly signed a lease providing the entire Minnehaha Park area for the venture. In early August of 1917, preliminary incorporation papers were signed for a moving picture production studio to be established at Spokane with capitalization of $500,000.

On Aug. 24, 1917, Spokane newspapers announced that the new corporation would be called the Washington Motion Picture Corporation.

Tyrone Power had signed a three-year retainer with the company. The studio itself was to be a reproduction of the famous Universal City Studios in Los Angeles.

But the most interesting news was yet to come — Spokane's new studio was to produce Bible stories for the silent screen. On Aug. 27, 1917, the *Spokane Press* carried the following article:

SPOKANE TO HAVE HUGE PICTURE PROJECT

A brand new industry, backed by millions of dollars and with the world for its market, is coming to town. This city is to become famous as the home of a tradition-breaking religious revolution. Spokane is to become the center of a continent-wide motion picture syndicate, financed, operated and owned exclusively by 125,000 churches in the United States and Canada.

On May 5, 1918, the *Spokane Press* announced that work had begun on Spokane's first motion picture. Tyrone Power, the leading man, had arrived the night before, and the first scenes were to be filmed on the Little Spokane River that day.

Although the Washington Motion Picture Corporation succeeded in erecting a significant studio at Minnehaha Park and at least one silent movie was made during Power's time in Spokane, his venture failed; funds from investors in New York never materialized, and they were unable to secure enough investors in the Spokane area.

Power gave up and went back to his family in Cincinnati. Following his departure, the city was left with an impressive but empty studio. Over the next few years, several other companies attempted to establish their business at the park, but none were successful — until Nell Shipman came to Spokane in 1920.

Shipman thought it was perfect. By now, she had accumulated a private zoo consisting of over 70 varieties of furry actors. It was time to make the break from Hollywood.

❖ ❖ ❖

Shipman arrived in Spokane with her crew and cast in the early spring of 1922. She described their accommodations in the following manner: "The Cast lived at Louis Davenport's lovely hotel and ate high on the hog. I marched in and out of an expensive suite in my leather coat, carrying my briefcase, playing Madame Producer to the hilt but scared cold-silly inside. Could *The Grub Stake* carry the load?"

One of Shipman's first challenges was raising money for the production and preparing the Minnehaha studio for her needs. Within a short time, they raised $180,000 to film a feature called *The Grub Stake*. She immediately hired three locals to begin construction of the necessary changes and accommodations she would need for her productions and animals. The men she hired were Paul Peters, a skilled carpenter and two of his sons, Lloyd and Ray. (Both sons had a desire to be movie actors and worked for Shipman as carpenters and actors for the duration of her stay in the Inland Northwest.)

Filming began almost immediately, with some of the first scenes being shot during March of 1922 near Tiger, Ione and upper Lake Thomas in Pend Oreille County. Other scenes were shot at the Minnehaha studio and on Mt. Spokane. An interesting event occurred during the Mt. Spokane filming, which appeared in the May 11, 1922 edition of the *Spokane Press*:

BITTEN BY A BEAR: Van Tuyle Saves Hand by Not Snatching It. The first accident of the season with the animals of the Nell Shipman zoo occurred yesterday on Mt. Spokane, when Brownie, the big bear which has been one of the tamest pets of the studio, attacked Bert Van Tuyle, manager, crushing the bones in his left hand and tearing the tendons so seriously that there is a chance it may be permanently crippled.

The accident occurred when the company was working "on location" at the top of Mt. Spokane. The bear had been worked all day and had become peevish. It crawled into a crevice, and Van Tuyle, in attempting to entice it to come out, extended his left hand. Brownie snapped at it, crushing it. The only thing that saved the manager from more serious injury, according to Russell Bankson, press agent for the company, was the fact that he did not attempt to snatch away his hand, but waited quietly until the bear released it.

Physicians who attended the injured man state that it will be at least a couple of weeks before he can use it, but they expect the tendons to grow together eventually. The bear has been muzzled and tied since the accident.

This was not Van Tuyle's first poor judgment call. During a nighttime filming session in Canada of *Back to God's Country*, he wore insufficient footgear for the 60-degree-below-zero weather, causing frostbite to one of his feet. Even worse, he ignored the symptoms until he nearly went mad from the pain and eventually had to have several of his toes amputated. This injury would plague him the rest of his life.

❖ ❖ ❖

In 1922, Shipman moved her production company and zoo to the northern end of Priest Lake, where she built a studio and movie camp called Lionhead Lodge. She described her affinity for the area and the trip there in her autobiography:

> *Did you ever come to a place and instantly recognize it as your Ultima Thule, the one spot in all God's world where you belonged, where your roots could go deep into soil which would forever nourish you, where inspiration and spiritual blessing welled up from the earth to top the tallest Tamarack, spread to encasing bowl of sky, return on every waterway to feed you everlastingly? Such a spot, so it seemed to me, was Priest Lake in Idaho.*
>
> *We reached it by rail to the town of Priest River, then by car to Coolin on the shore and from there by hired motorboat up the lake to its north end where a narrow water-lane snaked its way to Upper Priest Lake and was called the Thorofare.*

The studio was in existence from 1922 to 1925. During that time, Shipman experienced some of the greatest extremes in happiness and suffering in her life. *The Grub Stake* was completed, but the American distributor who purchased it soon declared bankruptcy, tying the film up in legal actions. Unable to pay her investors and creditors, her quality of life began to decline. The little band of maverick moviemakers continued to produce other small films, but struggled with many hardships, including the extremely harsh winter of 1923-1924. As 1924 wore on, Van Tuyle who had possessed a rather flamboyant personality, commanding respect from most who knew him, became increasingly cantankerous and unpredictable as a result of his frostbite injury. His resulting reactions to those around him had a detrimental effect on the studio.

Shipman reached her breaking point at Christmas 1924 and, with her son Barry, now age 12, left Priest Lake for the last time. Her departure coincided with the end of her relationship with Bert Van Tuyle. What remained of her zoo was donated to a zoo in San Diego. During the time she spent in the Inland Northwest, she gained tremendous notoriety and left a favorable impression on most all she touched. The traumatic circumstances under which she abandoned the studio left many creditors who were never paid off, the majority of whom didn't mind. They had the honor of knowing this hardworking, decent woman who had met with a run of bad luck.

Leaving Priest Lake and her beloved studio and zoo spelled the death of Nell Shipman's acting and movie producing career. She did continue to be active on the fringes of the film industry, writing scripts, stories and novels, for the rest of her life. She married again and, although the relationship was not long lasting, the union produced twins — a boy and a girl. Shipman died and was buried at Cabazon, California, in 1970 at the age of 77. Her gravestone is a small, inconspicuous granite reminder of her. It simply reads: "NELL SHIPMAN, FINI 1970." In 1977 the State of Idaho dedicated the location of Lionhead Lodge on Priest Lake as Shipman Point in her honor. ■

Joe Peirone, with his new truck at his parents' house in Garden Springs, circa 1938.

Joe Peirone's First Truck

BY TED S. McGREGOR JR.

First published in the *Inlander* on March 4, 2010

PROLOGUE: The Lewiston Run, 1938

Somehow, young Joe Peirone got a truck. They weren't easy to come by smack in the middle of the Great Depression, but just a few years after graduating from Lewis and Clark High in 1934, Joe managed to grab a foothold on life that could haul a couple tons. In those days, a truck was the difference between the bread lines and pulling your own weight.

In an early entrepreneurial burst, with just enough cash hoarded to make a play, he grabbed his brother-in-law Frank and made a trip that might have gone something like this:

Joe had heard about a little orchard down outside Lewiston, so they set out one July morning, navigating the harrowing 65 switchbacks down the Lewiston Grade. The grower pointed to the boxes and ladders; it was up to Joe and Frank to pick and pack their crop.

Passing through the rolling Palouse on the way home, their precious cargo filled the road ahead with American Dreams getting more plausible by the mile.

Joe was in the driver's seat of a going concern.

Up in Spokane, in the wholesale district along Stevens Street between First and Second, they pulled the truck into a spot as close as they could get to the action. First thing in the morning, grocers from all over the city would shop along produce row to stock their stores. Joe and Frank unloaded their scarlet booty and set up a little display on the sidewalk — Joe handed out samples. "Yes, sir, these here are the first cherries of the season."

Box by box, dollar by dollar, the truck emptied out. They sold the last lots to fruit wholesalers at a discount — those cherries wouldn't last forever. Like his dad always told him, the produce business is a race against time.

After three days away, Joe pulled into the driveway of his two-room house late that night; the rattle of his truck woke his new young wife, Alice. She found him in standing in the kitchen — a flat of beautiful red cherries on the counter, a wad of cash next to it, a weary grin on Joe's face. They laughed at the improbability of it all until the tears came. They ate those cherries 'til their stomachs ached.

That fruit never tasted sweeter.

Joe's Life

That Lewiston run was just the beginning for Joe Peirone. A few years later, he founded Peirone Produce, and now, 65 years later, his firm is expanding and moving into one of the nation's most high-tech produce distribution centers — triple the space it currently occupies.

Joe, who passed away in 1992, a few years after selling his company to Spokane's URM, would be proud of the new building — he'd want to see the plans to make sure they'd be taking good care of the bananas and tomatoes.

Lots of businesses expand, build new headquarters, launch new products; Joe's story isn't so different. But Joe's life is evocative of so many of the people who survived the Great Depression and helped build the Inland Northwest and enable this unprecedented quality of life.

We owe it to them not to forget what they did.

People like Joe — people who generally minded their own business and kept their heads down working — people like that never get much notice in newspaper stories. I've always thought that was a shame. So here we are, putting Joe's life in the newspaper.

I hope Joe's life resonates with you. It's inspiring to remember that small dreams like his can grow — and even help launch new ones.

Yes, I knew Joe Peirone. To me, he was always just "Grandpa."

❖ ❖ ❖

To really get to know Joe, first you have to meet his dad, Dominic. Joe's opportunities, slim as they might have been in the mid-1930s, came on the power of his father Dominic's determination. Facing a lack of opportunity in a nation seemingly adrift, Dominic became one of 9 million Italians who immigrated to America between the 1870s and 1920s. In early 1903, Dominic left his family home in Rifreddo, Italy — a village nestled along the foothills of the Western Alps, closer to Marseilles than Rome.

According to the Ellis Island Archives, Dominic arrived at the Port of New York on March 10, 1903. Apparently, he made the journey with friends, as there were four other men from Rifreddo listed on the manifest of the 1,100-passenger *Le Bretagne*.

In those days, you needed a sponsor to immigrate, and the boys from Rifreddo had some kind of Italian brethren in Mellen, Wisconsin, so they set out for northern Wisconsin. Dominic was 23 years old and didn't speak English.

Today Mellen has fewer than 1,000 residents, and Dominic worked building furniture there for a time, but he didn't stay long. Family anecdotes have it that after a night too close to 60 degrees below zero, he decided to move West.

In those days, capitalists had lots of great notions that took lots of manpower to pull off. A big one was starting right around the time Dominic was looking to improve his lot — the newly incorporated Potlatch Corporation was building the biggest sawmill in the world just downstream from the biggest stand of white pine on the planet in north central Idaho.

By 1905, he could have ridden either the Great Northern or the Northern Pacific; both lines had their eastern terminus in the Twin Cities. But on his way out to Potlatch, he passed through Spokane. While switching trains, he would have seen a bustling city feeding the labor needs of the mines, the farms and the timber mills. If he looked closer, he might have appreciated the crowning cliffs of basalt and the fertile valley he passed through just before pulling into the station.

Potlatch was to be one of those planned work communities — a place on the other end of the spectrum from the ramshackle work camps that usually sprang up around the latest exercise in natural resource extraction. Maybe it was too many men or too rigid a world, with company stores not quite living up to Dominic's vision of American freedom.

Whatever the reason, Dominic left Potlatch to put down deeper roots in that nice little city he saw on his way out West. He'd settle in Spokane.

❖ ❖ ❖

By the late 1900s, perhaps with money he saved from his days at the mill, Dominic bought a little piece of land in West Central Spokane.

In Spokane, Dominic tapped into skills he learned in Italy and started working as a stonemason. Using local basalt, he created birdbaths he'd sell at Manito Park on the weekends; he also did rockwork for some of those fancy new mansions going up on the South Hill. In his off hours, he built a brand new house of his own at 2008 W. Carlisle Ave., now torn down to make way for Audubon Elementary.

But his house was not a home yet. To finish the job, Dominic would need to get back on that transcontinental railroad.

Across the sea, Dominic, now 29, might have handed out Wrigley's or some other proof of America upon his return to Rifreddo. He'd have certainly worn his best, wanting to show that, eight years in, this adventure was agreeing with him.

After greeting the family and answering questions from visitors all over the valley, he met her. The girl he remembered only as a shy 9-year-old was all grown up now — and betrothed to him. His letters must have been convincing, as Dominic and his parents won the consent of Caterina's parents.

Caterina was 17.

The newlyweds retraced Dominic's original path back to Spokane and moved into their new home in the summer of 1911. After the whirlwind subsided and Dominic was back to work, Caterina sat alone and cried — this she told me when she was in her 80s and I was a teenager. She couldn't speak the language; other young wives laughed at her, and the shopkeepers cheated her. She missed home. But after the tears ran out, she set her mind to making something of their new life in America.

It wasn't long before the couple moved to a lightly settled area in Garden Springs, west of downtown, where they could have gardens, like back home. You can still see the family homes, built by Dominic, out there on Lawton Road.

Soon there were kids on the way — little Clara was born and then, on Jan. 15, 1915, along came Guiseppe Pietro Peirone. That was his proper

Italian name, but as a natural-born American, they'd call him Joe.

❖ ❖ ❖

For the growing Peirone family — little brothers Henry and Julius and sister Mary came along after Joe — farming was a way of life, just as it was for their relatives back in Italy.

"My grandfather had huge truck gardens," recalls Joe's daughter (and my own mom), Jeanne, of the elaborate rows of vegetables the family would harvest and sell at markets in Spokane. "They made a living off their gardens up there. I remember my grandma got up at 3:30 in the morning to work in the gardens in the summertime."

So it's no surprise that when the time came to strike out on his own, Joe stuck to what he knew — buying and selling fruits and vegetables. But it wasn't an auspicious time to enter the workforce. Like the rest of the world, Spokane was suffering under the ravages of the Great Depression; unemployment was around 25 percent, but that didn't stop trainloads of drifters from coming to the city to look for work. They were called drifters because if they couldn't find work in a month, Spokane ordinances required them to move on.

So it must have seemed unlikely, indeed, at that moment when Joe kicked the tires on that first truck, but he would take the produce business to a whole new level.

First Joe became a trucker, hauling for the outfits down around the Stevens Street warehouse district. In the summer he'd be running to Wenatchee; in the winter, he'd head for California. Most of the produce guys took their meals at the Silver Inn across the street from the warehouses — not to be confused with the swankier Silver Grill a block away inside the Hotel Spokane.

Joe liked more than the weak coffee — one waitress caught his eye, and an extravagant tip turned into a brief courtship. He and Alice were married in June of 1938; she was 18.

It probably didn't take long for Joe to notice that the job to have in the produce world was as a wholesaler — the middleman between the buyer and the seller. Getting that first truck was a start, and the Lewiston run proved he could do it. And soon he got a chance to prove he could do it every day.

In late 1944, Joe took over New Deal Produce, one of the lesser players in the wholesale district, but, still, a fixture there since 1934. Peirone Produce got off to a humble start — in fact, it barely had an address. That first warehouse was located at 171½ S. Stevens, and Bud Skredzvig laughs when asked what it was like. Bud, now 87, joined the business in 1946 and was Joe's right-hand man (and near-daily lunch companion) for the rest of his career.

"It wasn't what you would think of as an office," says Bud. "It was along the back wall of a filling station there on Stevens. There was a ramp that went down into a little garage. That was it."

But it was a start.

❖ ❖ ❖

Joe was drafted in May 1945, just as the War in Europe was ending. Maybe it was his flat feet or his two kids and a business, but he was never inducted. Instead, he got to work, making friends in the neighborhood — there was Archie, the new proprietor of Sanders Market up on Washington — and with growers and grocers. In those days, grocers often had to track down items on their own, with chaotic pricing to match. Grocers couldn't put up with the uncertainty and the hassle; the produce business needed to change.

Those were days of trial and error — lots of error, recalls Bud Skredzvig.

"There were lots of times when Joe was broke and he knew it, but he wouldn't admit it," recalls Bud. "Jean [Bud's wife, and the company bookkeeper], she'd get out the payables — they had a stack of the damn things — and they'd decide which they could pay now and which they would have to borrow on."

Joe himself recalled those times in a 1982 article in the industry newspaper *The Packer*: "We borrowed and borrowed again from the banks," Joe said. "It was hard to put enough money together to get business against the established companies."

Bud says it went beyond the banks — Joe borrowed money from Archie, the grocer up the street, and even one of his employees who had saved up a little.

"He had some mighty rough times getting going," says Bud, adding that Joe always paid back every cent he borrowed. And later, when the company got on solid footing, they paid every bill within a week.

For Joe, work and family were always combined, which brought its own complications. "Joe sure put up with a lot," Bud says.

But Joe needed any help he could get, and family stuck together. Frank Pignanelli, who was married to Joe's older sister Clara and was there for that first trip to Lewiston, slipped in and out of Peirone Produce. But he did finish his working life there in remarkable fashion: For more than 30 years, Frank babysat the bananas — checking their temperature and ripeness twice a day, six days a week. He followed the routine until he was 94 years old.

Joe's younger brother Julius was a buyer, brother-in-law Fain worked on the trucks, and his son, Jim, first went to work at the warehouse when he was 10 years old, ultimately holding pretty much every job Peirone Produce had to offer. Even his father Dominic worked there until he was 75, just a year before he passed away.

Oddly enough, a swipe of a bureaucrat's pen brought the next big change to the produce business. Sometime in 1950, Bud recalls, Second Avenue was turned into a one-way street. This made it impossible to turn trucks around to get into the Stevens Street wholesale district. It's as vacant today as it quickly became then — only a lone brick building remains in a sea of parking lots, just across the street from Allied Security.

❖ ❖ ❖

The next brilliant step was to co-locate all the produce companies under one roof — to replicate the bustle of Stevens Street, with better access and high hopes. It was almost an instant disaster.

The Produce Terminal, on Ide Street just along the northwest side of the Monroe Street Bridge, tried to recreate a past that wasn't really working. Grocers didn't show up to buy direct — they wanted deliveries, and the smart companies would need to accommodate them. It was also a bit of a den of thieves — too many people, too much temptation to pilfer. It reminded Joe of the centralized produce market he visited in Chicago, riddled with organized crime. And pricing got so cutthroat, nobody could actually make any money.

It took them until 1953, but they got out of the Produce Terminal as quickly as they could.

Their next stop wasn't exactly what you'd call fancy, but it would give them plenty of space to store produce, to load and unload their growing fleet of trucks and, best of all, it was far away from their competition. They moved into the shuttered Golden Age Brewery, which had been the Schade Brewery way, way back and the Hotel De Gink during the Depression. It's still standing today, looming high above the growing University District east of downtown Spokane.

This was the time Peirone Produce started turning the corner. Bud and Joe would travel to Tacoma to see how Pacific Coast Fruit did it. It was all about inventory control, Bud recalls the epiphany. The following Monday morning, they adopted several practices they saw on their trip.

This is where the frugality born in the Great Depression came in handy. Nothing went to waste — bins of potatoes were sorted to save the few that still had shelf-life in them, and they hired their own mechanics to maintain their growing fleet of trucks. (This was an ethic deeply ingrained; I remember dropping by to visit Joe and Alice one weeknight to see them sitting down to a meal of chicken necks. Nothing should go to waste.)

It was also a time to solidify the relationships that made his business run. Despite still being the smaller, underdog shop, he worked to win new business. He had his eye on one go-getter in particular — Mert Rosauer, who had opened Spokane's first-ever "super" market in 1949 at Third and Oak (where the Browne's Addition Rosauers still stands).

❖ ❖ ❖

Starting in the summer of 1952, Joe moved the family to Fresno for two months each summer. That arrangement, under the baking Fresno sun, continued for seven summers. Joe spent his days in the fields of central California with the growers who would supply him with tomatoes, cantaloupes, lettuce and so much more. He had gotten to know the apple growers and others around the Northwest during his days driving a truck, and he needed to know these people, too. His business depended on California. Many became more than business partners — they became his lifelong friends.

During the mid-1950s, Joe and Alice settled into family life. They added on to the two-room Garden Springs house his father had given him; he planted a cherry and apple orchard in the field between his house and his parents', and he built a greenhouse so he could grow starts in the winter to plant his own geraniums around the yard come springtime. The couple didn't travel much — they never did get over to Rifreddo.

Joe was pretty much always on the job, working six days a week, recalls

Jeanne: "I think my dad really had a lot of stress. He'd get phone calls from the truck drivers at all hours, letting him know they had a problem, or that they spilled a truck somewhere."

But in 1956 he did buy a cabin on Lake Coeur d'Alene. For years after that, Joe and Alice spent most of the free time they had out there.

The business was evolving quickly in the 1950s. Jim Peirone remembers the day in 1958 when Peirone Produce's very first self-contained refrigerated trailer rolled onto the lot.

"You always had to worry about perishables," Jim says. "That was always critical. And the early trucks didn't have much insulation. They had an ice bunker, with ten 300-pound blocks of ice, and a blower. You always had to unload the trucks right when you got them."

This gleaming new Freightliner was a game-changer.

Meanwhile, Joe's old friend Mert was going gangbusters. After some discussions, Joe and Mert shook hands in 1961 and struck a deal that would bind the two companies for the next 50 years. Peirone Produce would be the exclusive supplier to Rosauers supermarkets, but they would have to deliver to wherever they expanded — a deal that would ultimately send Peirone Produce trucks well into Montana.

Joe got what he'd always wanted; now he just had to keep up with his success.

❖ ❖ ❖

In December 1965, just 100 yards from their location in the old brewery, Peirone Produce opened its new, then-state-of-the-art, 23,000-square-foot warehouse — built almost identically to the plan used by Pacific Coast Fruit in Tacoma.

Jim Peirone remembers the 20 years that followed as the time when the team really dialed things in.

"We all worked together, and we were very, very successful at it," says Jim. "It was a very, very good business, and a career for lots of people."

I walked into this moment one summer morning in 1978. Joey Rubino handed me a broom and I was off, at age 15, to the first of nine summers working in the warehouse, doing everything from sorting potatoes to unloading banana trucks. Once I turned 18, I even joined the union and became a Teamster.

Joey was the merry prankster of the team and just one of the many

Italians who worked at Peirone's. There was Leo Dieni, Ernie Fruci — it was kind of Little Italy. (For the record, "Peirone" sounds like "purr-ohn"; under no circumstances were you *ever* to pronounce it like "Peironi." Maybe sounding too Italian was still a sore subject for Joe, having grown up Italian in a town run by the Irish.)

Ultimately, Peirone Produce allowed some long-timers of Irish descent — guys like Bob Casey and Pat Fitzpatrick, who started at age 17.

Any business is only as successful as its people allow it to be, and Peirone Produce has always been about the people who worked there — and who work there still.

"There was damn little turnover," says Jim Peirone. "Everybody was treated like family."

I still think about how important it was for me to learn how to put my head down and just get a job done — and I learned it from some of the best, and it did feel like a family.

"It was the definition of honest work," says my brother Jer, who also worked at the warehouse during the summertime. "The people I worked with worked hard, and being Joe's grandson, I had to work hard, too. I learned that work ethic, and I got to be around a functioning business and see that it takes everyone doing their part."

❖ ❖ ❖

By the 1980s, Joe and his team had succeeded in bringing the produce business into the modern era, creating order where there had been chaos. They helped solve a basic need of modern life — getting good food onto people's tables. But things would change yet again. In 1984, URM bought Rosauers, putting the handshake deal into question. United Retail Merchants has an even longer history than either Rosauers or Peirone, as it was founded by local folks in 1921 right here in Spokane; URM's founders had to overcome the same kinds of struggles as Joe and Mert.

By 1986 a deal had been struck, and Joe sold his company to URM; he stayed on for another year to help ease the transition. (When Jim Peirone retired in 1998, he was the last Peirone on the job.)

During that transition year, Joe trained URM's man, Pat Davidson, who became president and CEO of Peirone Produce. One early decision was to keep the name.

"What Peirone Produce had in place was probably the finest reputation in the industry," says Davidson. "It was very, very important to me that we maintain that name and the image associated with that name. It's still the same company as it was 40 years ago when Joe was building it."

In this era with growing recognition of the importance of strong local economies, it's worth remembering that some of the oldest names in town — URM, Rosauers, Peirone Produce — are all homegrown success stories that continue on today.

"I'm so proud of the fact that the name lingers on," says Jeanne. "My dad worked so hard for so many years."

And now it's time to move again, and you can blame the traffic, as when Peirone had to move from Stevens Street in 1950. Their current building, on land owned by Washington State University, is getting squeezed out by plans to expand the University District. Then there's the fact that they're bursting at the seams, with 100 employees, 40 trucks and a product line that seems to be growing every day, featuring bagged lettuce and other exotics only dreamed of in Joe's day. The new facility, located on Hallett Road off I-90 on the West Plains, will be almost triple the size of their current space.

"The new facility is absolutely state of the art," says Davidson, "with all of the latest technology that's available for refrigeration. It's the newest produce distribution building on the West Coast within the last 10 years."

They're moving in this month, 107 years to the month after Dominic Peirone set eyes on the Statue of Liberty and had to wonder how it would all end up.

❖ ❖ ❖

What can we learn by digging into family history? Of course it's humbling to learn more about the sacrifices that gave us our chance. And now that my brother Jer and I have a business together, it all makes more sense. Our own experiences make it easier to understand how hard it was for Joe.

But as I dug into my grandfather's life, I found something else — a common thread. At crucial moments throughout the story, people took risks to help each other when they needed it most. Everything hinged on the faith of family and the kindness of friends, and that's something we all need to remember as we live our own lives.

How did poor, young Dominic afford passage to America all those years ago? When my parents visited Rifreddo, they learned something new: A generous aunt loaned him the money to start a new life.

Where did Joe, a kid from a poor immigrant family, get the money to buy that first truck? There's no record or story, but it seems likely that his dad helped him with a down payment. Then, during his leanest years, Joe only stayed in business by borrowing from friends. His friend Mert Rosauer even took out a loan from his parents to launch his dream in 1934.

When we were ready to start the *Inlander*, we followed in that long tradition. We needed help, and by help we meant money. And we were asking for a lot of money to risk on what might rightly be described as a hare-brained scheme — to start a second newspaper… *in Spokane!* (We found out later this was essentially the line of reasoning a family adviser used to argue against our loan request.)

I had a sketch of a business plan, but the day I nervously presented it, my prospective lender didn't even bother to look at it. She answered my awkward pitch without a moment's hesitation: "Of course."

Soon I had a cashier's check in my hand. The signature at the bottom of that check? Alice Peirone.

That was in 1993, just a year after Joe had passed away. Our first issue of the *Inlander* came out a few months later; Joe just missed it.

And when Jer says, "There is no *Inlander* without Peirone Produce," he means that our debt goes well beyond that seed money. Of course we learned from our parents, but the lessons of Joe's life rubbed off on us, too — the perseverance it took for him to build his company; the personal touch that fueled his success; and the selflessness of doing what he did (and what Dominic did before him) to make things better for the generations ahead.

Thanks, Grandpa.

EPILOGUE: Behind Sanders Market, 2010

Since the cavemen first gazed up at the stars, we've all been yearning to know where we came from, why we're here and where it's all going. Genealogy is such an obsession because it tackles these mysteries in ways that touch our souls.

We experience the world through our own eyes; all history is personal. And as I walked around the old neighborhood down on Stevens Street, where so much of this story happened, I was feeling those existential pangs.

Remember Archie? Joe's friend who ran Sanders Market just across the street from Peirone Produce back in the 1940s? Well, I left something out about him. I didn't mention his last name.

It was McGregor.

Years after they were neighbors, one summer day in 1961, Joe stopped into his old friend Archie's new store in Coeur d'Alene (at the old Lakeview Court across from the City Park). Joe had his daughter Jeanne with him. Archie's son, Ted, was home from college working in his dad's store that day.

Their eyes met. A phone call, a date and a few years later, Ted added the Sr. to his name.

So I'm here today, able to pour this story into my computer, because my two grandfathers went into business a block away from each other.

As I stood out in the alley behind the old Sanders Market, I looked straight up into the same sky they toiled under. I thought of Joe and Frank pulling up after their run down to Lewiston. I thought of Archie on his first day behind the counter at Sanders, only months after getting back from the war. I imagined my grandfathers sharing a beer some night before heading home to their families, talking about nothing in particular.

As I looked back down, it was 2010 again, but my feet felt heavier somehow — just a little more rooted into the ground below. ■

Spokane's own Bing Crosby redefined the holiday season with his song, "White Christmas."

A Bing Crosby Christmas

BY WILLIAM STIMSON

First published in the *Inlander* on December 25, 2003

The Bing Crosby Centennial this year put me in a somber mood. The celebration of Bing's 100th birthday itself was fun — the flattery of hearing that people came from as far as England and South America to see Spokane, and so on. But for me it brought on the churn of emotions one feels at a wedding in the family: Despite all the fun and smiles, you can't shake the sad feeling that someone is leaving home.

Until he died in 1977, Spokane could claim Bing himself. He grew up in the yellow house up the street. He mentioned Spokane in interviews. Lots of people in town had known him and could tell funny stories about him.

Now time has passed and we have a "centennial." No matter how you package 100 years, it only connotes remoteness.

I brooded about this for months after the centennial celebration. Then finally I had a thought that made me feel better. We have been focusing on how a hometown boy made good. What gets a lot less attention is the other side of the equation, and the part that might be most instructive to a town of a famous son, namely: *How* a hometown makes a boy good.

❖ ❖ ❖

One cannot read Gary Giddins superb new biography, *Bing Crosby: A Pocketful of Dreams*, without being impressed by how this average Spokane kid was coddled by his community. Crosby's father was a low-paid bookkeeper. Yet his family lived in a roomy house of their own on a wide street that connected all seven Crosby kids with almost unlimited opportunities.

Spokane and the Gonzaga neighborhood were so organized as to give a kid like Bing Crosby any kind of future he should aspire to. One of Bing's close pals, Ralph Foley, for example, went on to be a judge and father of a Speaker of the U.S. House of Representatives. Another of Bing's gang, Frank Corkery, would become president of Gonzaga University. Yet another friend, Ray Flaherty, became one of the great stars of the National Football League.

Bing himself took a liking to the stage and elocution. As he said himself, he had endless opportunities in school functions and other contests to flex these talents. "I won a couple of awards with Horatius and Spartacus," Crosby recalled in his autobiography. "I took those eloquent lines in my teeth and shook them as a terrier shakes a bone." He took part in plays and debates, but "the elocution contests were the big events. They were held in the parish hall and everybody in the parish came."

There's a good example of how a community stands behind its youth. It sits patiently in front of them while they make their awkward attempts to develop skills.

Notwithstanding the fact that he had little money and no scholarships, Crosby could aspire to a college education and a career in law. This was a present of the Jesuit fathers and many a protestant local booster who helped them open Gonzaga three decades earlier. As a consequence, Spokane sent forth a certain type of entertainer.

According to Giddens: "Bing Crosby is the only major singer in American popular music to enjoy the virtues of a classical education. It grounded his values and expectations, reinforcing his confidence and buffering him from his own ambition. As faithful as he was to show business, his demeanor was marked by a serenity that suggested an appealing indifference. He had something going for him that could not be touched by Hollywood envy and mendacity."

His philosophical education went on beyond the classroom. Bing was rambunctious and occasionally rebellious — the kind of liberty-seeking adolescent portrayed in his 1940s movies *Going My Way* and *The Bells of St. Mary's*. In Spokane, Bing was corralled by a tolerant and wise network of neighborhood parents, coaches, once or twice by policemen, and especially by the very sort of Fathers O'Malley that Bing had portrayed in the movies.

❖ ❖ ❖

The most remarkable thing about the celebrity Bing Crosby, aside from his singing, was his humor. This, too, surely owed something to the old neighborhood. Many of the people in the neighborhood were, like Crosby himself, Irish, second and third generation mostly, and there is just something about the Irish personality that wants to smirk.

I can testify to this because I grew up in Crosby's neighborhood — four decades later — and I saw it and suffered from it 10,000 times. Spoofing and chiding were the tone of the neighborhood. The simplest thing, ordering a hamburger, say, becomes the occasion for verbal byplay over whether one's onions were a shame to the human race. I remember being in the University Drug Store and watching on as the proprietor, Bill Stevens, rang up a line of purchasers. "Thank you, Mr. Stevens," said Mr. McGinn, taking his package. "And I just hope this time you gave me the right medicine! Boy was I sick that last time!" Stevens was taken aback, as were the customers in line, clutching their own prescriptions, and I was the only one who could see Mr. McGinn grinning as he headed for the door.

It was in Bill Stevens' drug store that I first discovered that the singer of "White Christmas" was thinking of the old neighborhood. I picked up a magazine from the rack and read one of those "The Stars Tell of Their Favorite Christmases" articles, and Bing recalled snow-filled trees and sledding down Sharp Avenue hill. That was where I had just been!

After Crosby sang "White Christmas" in 1942, according to *The Great American Christmas Almanac*: "Snow... became more important to the general Christmas scene than it had ever been before; it became essential. And that is why you have to have it annually in Puma, Ariz., simulated in rolls of white cotton... It no longer looks incongruous to anyone; we will have our White Christmas, no matter where we are or what the weatherman says."

Of course, Irving Berlin had New York City in mind when he wrote the lines of "White Christmas." But the sincerity in Crosby's voice when he sang of Christmases "just like the ones I used to know" certainly came from Spokane.

This is significant because "White Christmas" became "the anthem of Christmas sentiment," as one critic put it. It became the favorite Christmas song of 1942 and never lost that position. It has sold more than 31 million copies and counting.

Before "White Christmas," Crosby's 1935 record of "Silent Night" and, on the flip side, "Adeste Fideles," were the best-selling Christmas carols. He considered these sacred songs and refused to record them for commercial distribution until he eased his conscience by ceding all profits to charities.

"Bing was downright cowed by 'Silent Night,'" according to Giddins. Perhaps that was because he had first heard it intoned by 100 voices under the high dome of St. Aloysius Church at Midnight Mass. I suspect so because as a kid I walked down the same street as he did on Christmas Eve to go to midnight Mass. To me, "Silent Night" will always be that experience of stepping into the mysterious winter night and walking under snow or a roving winter moon toward the church steeples, past the mute nativity scene outside the church, then into the cavernous Church, alive with incense, candles and otherworldly voices, "…all is calm, all is bright…"

❖ ❖ ❖

Since he first recorded "Silent Night" in 1935, Bing Crosby has remained the undisputed chief caroler of American Christmas. Why is that? No one can say what makes an aesthetic difference. Possibly, though, Bing Crosby, like many artists (including Charles Dickens, Mark Twain and Robert Frost), searched for deeper meaning in the deep wells of childhood experience.

If so, there's a satisfying role for a hometown. Crosby did something to add to Christmas and — by doing something to improve Crosby — so did Spokane. ∎

The Crescent Department store, circa 1952.

Remembering Spokane in the 1950s

First published in the *Inlander* on December 20, 1995

JACK GERAGHTY

When I was a kid growing up in Spokane, what a let-down it was when my cousins would come over from Seattle.

I would say, "Isn't Mt. Spokane something?" They would counter with, "We have Mt. Rainier."

I would say, "Look at the Spokane River — ever seen so much water?" They would rejoin, "We have Elliott Bay, Lake Washington and the Puget Sound."

I would say, "Let's go visit Manito Park and the Duncan Gardens." They would reply, "We have Volunteer Park and the Woodland Park Zoo."

So it was with some delight in the early 1950s that I finally could get back at these residents of Magnolia Bluff, with their snobbish airs and local Magnolia neighborhood movie theater, by taking them to a showing of *Ali Baba and the Forty Thieves* at my new neighborhood theater — the Garland.

In that time, the Garland was a big deal in Spokane — our first movie theater outside of the downtown. It wasn't a 10-screen complex, just a great neighborhood movie house that actually attracted people from all over Spokane.

Before the Garland, we went to movies (pre-television, of course) at the art-deco Fox (one screen only), the State (now the Met), the Bandbox, the Orpheum, the Liberty, the Grenada (later the first home of the Civic Theatre) and the Post Street — not to mention the somewhat seedy Rialto, Rex and Nu-Rex, all located in Spokane's infamous skid row area.

Movies were where kids and grownups (when they weren't listening to the *Lux Radio Theater* or the Jack Benny and Bob Hope radio shows) got a lot of their entertainment in Spokane in those days. From *Fantasia* to *Eagle Squadron* to *Going My Way* — we saw a lot of movies. (Maybe it was because Spokane had, and has more than its share of Catholics or that Bing Crosby was from here, but *Going My Way* and, later, *The Bells of St. Mary's* had an unusually long run at the old Liberty Theater. I saw *Going My Way* about five times, but a friend of mine from the old St. Francis of Assisi grade school days, Leo Chandler, had the record — 14 times!)

Here's some more about that Spokane of the 1950s — particularly the early part of that decade: There was no East-West I-90 freeway, so the Spokane Valley was perceived to be kind of a semi-agricultural area out in the sticks.

There was no North Town (though you could see it coming), no Shadle Center, only a few stores in Lincoln Heights — but Hillyard had a Mayor, albeit honorary, in George Brown.

Commercial airlines (Northwest, United and a fledgling airline known as West Coast, later Hughes AirWest, later PSA, etc., etc.) were beginning to fly out of Geiger Airport with its World War II barracks terminal. The Felts Field runway just wasn't long enough any more for the DC-4s, DC-6Bs and Stratocruisers. A big deal in our family in those days was a Sunday drive out to Geiger in our 1949 Kaiser sedan to watch the planes come and go.

As a teenager, growing up in Spokane in the early-1950s, there were many recollections for me beyond movies and airplanes. Here are some other highlights:

Going to high school then was a pretty simple situation. There was no Ferris or Shadle or St. George's. There was just North Central (my alma mater) and Lewis and Clark on the other side of the river where all the rich kids lived. (I actually went out with an LC cheerleader when I was a senior and was introduced to the South Side world, but that's another story.)

Now, before everyone else gets all excited, there actually were two other high schools in Spokane — Rogers and Gonzaga. (It wasn't "Prep" then, just Gonzaga.) They, of course, beat NC and LC pretty badly in football (the Gonzaga touchdown twins, Dick Sprague and Joe Lynch, pretty well could score anytime they wanted), but those schools didn't do so well in other sports.

From my point of view, the big rivalry then was between NC and LC.

Football games were played in the old Gonzaga University stadium (10,000 seats), then at Ferris Field baseball park near Playfair, and finally in 1951 at Albi Stadium. (What a big-time thing that seemed to be — something my Seattle cousins couldn't counter.)

Basketball games were played in the old National Guard Armory (now the site of LaserQuest), and the school spirit and rivalry was something else. In the NC vs. LC series, for example, the northsiders all wore dark blue civil war vintage U.S. Calvary caps while the southsiders wore the grey caps of the confederacy. It only added to the wildness.

Lewis and Clark under the coaching of the great Squinty Hunter won a lot of those games. Squinty's teams always seemed to be so much in control, so cool, so, well, South Side, that it was particularly gratifying when, as in 1952, North Central beat them and went to the State Tournament in Seattle. (All State Tournament games were played in Seattle then.)

There's a lot of talk from teenagers these days about not having anything to do. For some reason, that didn't seem to be the case in the early '50s.

There were the dances at the "Spot," located in the Odd Fellows Hall on West First. Looking back, those weekly dances to the tunes of Glen Miller, Tommy Dorsey and Fats Domino seem a little strange now. Everyone danced to what was called the "Rho Beta" step (Rho Beta was a social club at NC) and the girls danced together, with the boys cutting in. You were in real trouble if you didn't come with a friend (for cutting in), or if your friend wouldn't dance with the partner of the girl you wanted to dance with.

Hot spots on the North Side were the Triple X (Root Beer), Baker's Beacon drive-ins on North Division at the foot of the hill and Gage's Restaurant at Monroe and Northwest Blvd. All gone, now.

Kids with cars cruised Riverside, and for a real spooky time you could cruise Trent Alley, in the heart of the skid row area. Located just across from the present Opera House and Riverfront Park, it was just Trent then, not the grand "Spokane Falls Blvd." Trent and Main Avenues were the heart of the skid row.

Some other observations about those days include going to dinner at the Matador restaurant in the Davenport Hotel, still in its glory; going to the State Line in Idaho at places like the "First and Last Chance" where you could drink at 18 and also play the slot machines; hearing my parents talk about the private clubs (that, for a long time, were the only places where hard liquor was served) like the Athletic Roundtable and the Press Club; and also the coming of television to Spokane, with its small black-and-whites screen where you would watch such fascinating shows as wrestling, *The Boyle Fuel Talent Hour* and test screen patterns.

It was a much different world in Spokane in the 1950s — much different than today. Yet, some things remain the same. We're still caught in that swirling eddy, somewhere between a small farm town and a truly urban city. And we're still trying — from World's Fairs to new Arenas — to compete with our cousins to the West.

Jack Geraghty grew up to become the mayor of Spokane.

KITTY KELLEY

Looking back on the '50s in Spokane is like turning to a faded snapshot. Violence was not a daily concern, and nighttime was for making out, not murder. Life seemed simple and innocent. People left their doors unlocked, and only banks had alarm systems. Guns were reserved for the holsters of Roy Rogers and Hopalong Cassidy.

The images of growing up when Eisenhower was President and Princess Elizabeth became Queen are crystallized in my mind by pigtails, saddle shoes and layers of starched crinolines. I see men (grownups like my father and his friends) wearing snap-brim hats like Frank Sinatra when he sang "In the Wee Small Hours." Men tipped their hats to older women and to God (at least, my father always tipped his to Mr. Anthony's white-haired wife and toward the church).

During the '50s, women wore girdles, merry widows (corsets), nylons with seams and high heels called "spikes. They also wore hats and gloves to luncheons and bridge parties, and threw funny little furs with dangling mink paws around their shoulders to look glamorous.

You ask if Spokane, like Brigadoon, was out of touch, an overly protective place to grow up. Perhaps. Or, maybe it was just my own sheltered background. I recognize now that I grew up removed from reality, and pitifully ignorant. I was unaware of war, politics, civil rights. I was — I'm ashamed to admit — oblivious. I suppose I knew there were Republicans and Democrats, and that my parents were probably the former, only because the latter were always called "damn fools" as in "That damn fool Harry S. Truman."

My contact with the outside world came from books — I got my first library card when I was five — and radio. I remember going to bed early on Sunday nights to listen to Edgar Bergen and Charlie McCarthy, Our Gal Sunday, Helen Trent, Stella Dallas, Amos and Andy, The Shadow, The Whistler and The Great Gildersleeve.

And then came television. We whooped every week watching Phil Silvers con the army as Sergeant Bilko, and my mother took the phone off the hook so she would not be disturbed during *Robert Montgomery Presents*. She adored Groucho Marx making the duck come down to pay contestants on *You Bet Your Life*. I watched *The Eddie Fisher Show* and cried when he sang "Oh My Papa."

Most Americans move every five years, but I lived in the same house all my life — East 310 High Drive. Growing up on Harlan Boulevard, which later became High Drive, I hiked down the bluff to Hangman Creek followed by my dog. I picked buttercups and took walks with my father, who never left the house without his shillelagh.

I probably make Spokane sound like *The Donna Reed Show*, but I loved growing up there. I even loved the hideous green gabardine uniform I had to wear at Holy Names Academy. I saw Patrice Munsel perform at the Coliseum and Bing Crosby play golf at Hayden Lake. I have fond memories of ice skating at Cannon Hill, sledding at Manito, swimming at Comstock. I took dancing lessons from Mrs. West, drama lessons from Alice Garvin Windsor, piano lessons from Virginia Moore, and still can't perform.

I grew up having to get tick shots every summer to go to the lake, eating egg salad sandwiches at the counter at Greenough's, meeting friends under the clock at the Crescent and stopping at Mrs. Johnson's Bakery on Grand Boulevard for butterhorns every Sunday after church. I remember handing out Hostess cupcakes with Clarabell the Clown on the *Howdy Doody Show* at KREM-TV. I even remember buying penny candy.

So help me, God, I sound like Barney Fife describing Mayberry.

Kitty Kelley grew up to become the foremost unauthorized biographer of the 20th Century.

PAUL SANDIFUR JR.

People often think of the '50s as a kind of golden age and look back fondly on how things used to be. Spokane was indeed very different when I grew up here, but to my standards, it wasn't very idyllic. In fact, I think those who would like to return to Spokane in the '50s might be disappointed.

Spokane, especially downtown, was not a very beautiful place. Trent Avenue (the stretch that is now Spokane Falls Boulevard) was crowded with derelicts, many of whom were intoxicated to the point of passing out on the sidewalk. I remember having to step over them. I had a paper route nearby, and most of my customers had alcohol and money problems.

What is now Riverfront Park was ugly railroad yards and industrial plants, including dry cleaners that dumped their chemicals directly into the river. We were all warned never to go near the river as it was polluted. The city also dumped raw sewage into the river, and it smelled terrible.

In those days, prejudice was common. Most of the adults I knew were racially as well as religiously prejudiced. People seemed to have a narrow view of the world. I was kicked out of high school for three days because I brought up the subject of evolution in a biology class, and my civics teacher got into a lot of trouble for a class discussion on unions. It seemed to me the school was not big on freedom of expression. One day we had a student strike and everyone left school after the 2 pm break. We made the headlines the next morning.

Although the schools now have a reputation for not being safe, then, too, there was a lot of fighting in high school, especially racial disputes. Many of the boys carried knives, but I don't remember any guns.

Cars were a big thing, and we all wanted a fast car. There were some real powerful cars in those days, and we would drag race whenever we got a chance. We also cruised ("tooled") Riverside, a practice that continues today. I never found it a good way to meet girls, and I'm surprised it lasted so long.

We were all taught about drugs. Smoking and drinking were manly, but marijuana was terrible beyond description. I was always a little confused whether it just made you crazy and homicidal or if it would just kill you outright. After we tried it in the '60s, we were a little disappointed and somewhat skeptical about drug education.

Spokane wasn't much for culture in those days. Television was just coming in, but we didn't watch it often. It seemed we read more. Broadway plays did not come here, as they do now; neither were there many concerts or concert series.

On a positive note, there wasn't much crime. If someone was murdered, it was a big deal and got a lot of discussion. Now it seems almost daily fare in the papers. People were rarely burglarized and on the whole, I think, felt safer.

But we were all worried about atomic war. We had drills in school with the threat of swift and total extinction suspended over us like a heavy fog. That was a difficult way of growing up; it seemed then we might not reach adulthood at all.

Looking at the city now, I think Spokane has come a long way in the last 40 years. It is a much more beautiful city with the development of the Spokane River area and the creation of Riverfront Park — a green gem with sparkling falls in the city center.

In my view, culture is flourishing compared to what it was then. My company has supported the arts in Spokane, and today our community has several theaters, regular plays including Broadway musicals, and indoor and outdoor concerts the whole year through. In addition, there are several art galleries and museums in operation.

Overall, I think people are really more tolerant and have a broader outlook today. We have discovered there is a big world out there, and some are even willing to get involved. I am very proud of Spokane's progress. As a long-time resident of the area, I have seen it grow bigger and better and feel these are the good old days.

Paul Sandifur Jr. grew up to become president of Metropolitan Mortgage.

EDDIE CLARK

Spokane was a great place to grow up when I was one of the baby boomer kids being raised here starting in 1946. The Spokane of my youth was a fun, exciting place. My sister Katherine and I had the opportunity to be raised all over Spokane, criss-crossing the town from Hillyard to 17th and Ray, to Broadway and Nettleton, and then to 17th and Jefferson. We got to know a lot of kids in a lot of neighborhoods. We remember just about all of Spokane as "the old neighborhood."

Spokane seemed a lot bigger place then. The Valley was way far away, and Grandma used to take us "to Spokane" on the bus all the way from Hillyard. We learned the streets because the drivers called out the names when they stopped. One of my favorites was "Morton."

Instead of rollerblades, we had metal-wheeled skates; instead of 10-speeds with skinny tires, we had one-speeds with big balloon tires. We'd ride to the store for penny candy that really cost a penny — to Broadway Foods, Currie's, Peter Pan, Stejers, Heindselman's or to Doyle's Ice Cream.

If you had a dime, you could buy a cone or a "graveyard" at Doyle's — or 10 pieces of candy!

Natatorium Park was a magical place, our own Disneyland: the huge roller coaster; the carousel (thank heavens we saved it); the little Great Northern train that drove through the zoo; the octopus ride that upset stomachs; the very scary Spook House ride where you always knew what was there, but you were still scared anyway; the bumper cars; and the Strata-liner that you can still see at the pre-school on North Maple. The best days at Nat Park were at Shriners' picnics when every ride was free.

We saw Hopalong Cassidy and the Cisco Kid and Pancho at stadium shows (and the poor lady who fell off the sway pole and died before our eyes). Elvis was here, too. I saw him at Harley Reckard's House of Music in the Bon Marché and at the stadium, where silly, screaming kids picked up grass and dirt where the King had walked. We even watched stock car races in the stadium where the fastest driver of them all was named Sneva — Ed Sneva.

Before the Coliseum, we'd ice skate at the Elm Street Arena, or at Cannon Hill, Manito or Suicide ponds. When Tom Mableson, the voice of Spokane Hockey, formed the Spokane Americans youth hockey teams, we skated on the same Coliseum ice as our heroes, Tom Hodges, Gino Rozzini, Buddy Bodman, Emil "The Cat" Francis and Carl Cirullo.

Television was new and exciting, even if it was black and white. Ed Sullivan, Roy and Happy and Cisco and Pancho and Wild Bill and Zorro, Flash Gordon, Spin and Marty on *The Mickey Mouse Club*, Howdy Doody, Pinky Lee, Cap'n Cy and Popeye, and beautiful Miss Florence were some of our favorites. We learned Boyle Fuel's phone number from Stalit Stairway's singing twins — "Fairfax 8-1-5-2-1."

My first radio was a crystal set I made at scouts and our one BIG radio station was "K-N-E-W; Channel 79," playing early rock'n' roll with DJs "Frantic" Frank Herron and his "green inkers," "Addy Daddy Bobkins" and "Bubblehead" Bob. All the while we were growing up, we got all our news from Ross Woodward and Frank Hemingway on radio and Chet and David on TV. And the news didn't seem as bad as it is today. The Spokane of the '50s and '60s was a great place to raise kids. Lets all make sure that it still is today. ∎

Eddie Clark grew up to become an advertising executive. Now he goes by "Ed."

The Chad Mitchell Trio: (left to right) Mike Kobluk, Chad Mitchell and Joe Frazier.

Clean-Cut Radicals:
The Chad Mitchell Trio

BY MICK LLOYD-OWEN

First published in the *Inlander* on October 4, 2007

They looked innocuous enough when they started: Clean-cut, dressed in subdued suits and ties with nary a whisker on their youthful, beaming faces. There was none of that unwholesome stuff with the hips, either, like Elvis was doing — none of that devilish rock beat that was already poisoning the youth of the era. No, the Chad Mitchell Trio sang simple folk music — clear, confident voices ringing out with gutsy tremolo in pitch-perfect harmony. Their mothers must have been proud.

Yet the trio, formed in 1958 at Gonzaga University, made their name in the 1960s by means of an even more audacious tactic than a gyrating pelvis: Political satire. And in that moment between Elvis and the Beatles, the Chad Mitchell Trio was a fixture on the *Billboard* charts, powered by their commentary on social and political issues that crossed the boundary of what was acceptable at the time.

> *What did you learn in school today*
> *Dear little boys of mine?*
> *I learned that Washington never told a lie*
> *I learned that soldiers seldom die*

I learned that everybody's free
That's what the teacher said to me
And that's what I learned in school today
That's what I learned in school

I learned that policemen are my friends
I learned that justice never ends
I learned that murderers die for their crimes
Even if we make a mistake sometimes

I learned that wars are not so bad
I learned of the great ones we have had
We fought in Germany and in France
And someday I may get MY chance!

What did you learn in school today
Dear little boys of mine?
I learned our government must be strong
It's always right and never wrong
Our leaders are the finest men
And so we elect them again and again
And that's what I learned in school today
That's what I learned in school

It hardly seems subversive in 2007, when bands like Green Day excoriate the government with torrents of street-level verbiage that require their CDs to carry warning labels for parents. Yet many of the trio's songs were considered too controversial to be played on the radio — a trait that set them apart from other folk artists of their day.

"If you listened to some of this stuff today," says Chad Mitchell himself, "you'd wonder: What's wrong with that?"

Now, nearly 50 years after forming, the trio are back together, with Tom Paxton (who wrote the song above for the trio) and other members of the band, for a concert Saturday night.

So is "protest music" too strong a term for what the Chad Mitchell Trio became?

"No, I take it as a compliment," says Joe Frazier, one of the core members of the trio and a vital contributor to its political angle. "To *pro*test means to speak *for* something as well as against something, you know?"

The trio sang pointed songs about the hyper-conservative John Birch Society, about Barry Goldwater and the Vietnam War, about the draft, the KKK and racial integration in colleges — all without sounding whiny, bitchy or angry, as so much protest music later became. They also sang a broad assortment of more traditional folk songs about love, life, hurricanes and a "Marvelous Toy." They even tossed in a few gospel songs for good measure.

"We weren't avant-garde in any sense of political thinking," Mitchell says. "The more we sang and got involved in the material, the more educated [about social issues] we became. So in our case, we were kinda getting fed by the movement and feeding it back."

❖ ❖ ❖

The trio began with Gonzaga Men's Glee Club members Mitchell, Mike Kobluk and Brian Finnegan. Finnegan, who "didn't have time to go out and sing for beer money," according to Kobluk, dropped out and Mike Pugh took his place. A priest-in-training by the name of Reinard W. Beaver — a true believer, it would seem — had helped Mitchell book some engagements before and took an interest in the new trio. Heading to New York for Army chaplain school, Beaver invited the young trio to ride with him — "ostensibly, to sing on *The Ed Sullivan Show*," Kobluk says. "Of course, he had no contact with Ed Sullivan, and it wasn't until three to four years later that we finally did."

So the trio, like another famous Gonzaga student before them, packed into a car with Beaver and a guitarist and headed out of town with no money, no contacts and no plan. Beaver, full of faith, pitched the group's performance to anyone along the way who would listen.

"Like in Miles City, Montana, he heard a golf country club was having a meeting," Kobluk recalls, "and he would say, 'That's where we're singing tonight.' He'd go in and tell them he had this group out in the car who were on their way to New York to sing on *The Ed Sullivan Show*." Even when they balked, Beaver would talk them into it, Kobluk says. "What happened in Miles City was typical — we ended up with $50 to $60 more than we started with, and they called someone they knew to discount some motel rooms. So all of a sudden we had dinner, a few extra dollars and a place to stay that night."

New York proved to be more difficult than expected, but with the help of a literary agent who had connections in the entertainment industry, the trio got engagements and that all-important record deal.

"We didn't have the slightest idea what folk music was about," Mitchell says. "We were singers and didn't even play instruments. But everybody was looking for the next Kingston Trio, so we got lots of auditions."

Mitchell says the initial success of the Kingston Trio was considered by many in the industry to be a fluke until their second album, *From the Hungry I*, went gold. "They realized that this was a phenomenon — that the whole college market was hungry for this kind of entertainment."

Milt Okun, a music arranger/singer/producer who worked with Harry Belafonte, was brought in to help to polish the trio's sound. He became their music director and even something of a mentor. "Without him, we probably would never have been heard from again," Mitchell says.

The members, who actually wrote few of the songs they sang, credit Okun with helping to develop their social conscience and with charting their course by bringing them the music that defined what they became. They recorded as backup singers for Belafonte, sang on Pat Boone's TV show and lined up a tour with Bob Newhart.

At the same time, Pugh went back to school and the group picked up Joe Frazier, who had the strongest social and political convictions of any of them. He tugged the trio's helm even further to the port side.

❖ ❖ ❖

"My father was a steelworker, and I was raised in a working-class family," Frazier says, "so my own political opinions leaned rather hard to the left at an early age — 15, 16 years old."

Frazier admired the music of the Weavers, a folk band formed in 1948 that greatly influenced and inspired future folkies. The Weavers came under FBI investigation and were eventually blacklisted during the McCarthy era because of their support for labor unions and their leftist views. Member Pete Seeger had once belonged to the Communist Party of the United States. As a result of the blacklisting, radio stations terminated their airplay and the group virtually disappeared from public view.

"I think the Chad Mitchell Trio were direct descendants of the Weavers ideologically, politically and musically," Frazier says. "They were the generation before us. [Weavers member] Freddy Hellerman actually played on some of our albums with us and wrote some songs that we did, including one we'll be doing in Spokane: 'Business Goes on As Usual.'"

Frazier felt the sting of censure personally when he joined the Air Force, right out of high school. He auditioned for the Singing Sergeants — a military chorus — and was initially accepted. "Then I found out I wasn't," he says. "I was under investigation because of my politics. I was reading the wrong things, and saying the wrong things, and I ended up three months in the stockade." Considered a security risk even though he had broken no law nor done anything wrong, he was offered an "honorable" discharge — and after his imprisonment, he was ready to accept.

"If I was not a radical when I was put in the brig, I certainly was one when I got out," Frazier says. Fortunately, he then had funds from the G.I. Bill to do what he wanted to do in the first place: go to college. "I was a Christian at the same time, and I identified my Christianity — which has a lot to do with the poor and with peace — with my political opinions," Frazier says. "I didn't really see a difference or a conflict between them at all." An Episcopal priest since 1973, after his confessed "hippie period" in the late 1960s, Frazier still considers himself a protest person in what he preaches.

The trio, with Okun and Belafonte, sifted more than 150 hopefuls before they settled on Frazier as Pugh's replacement.

❖ ❖ ❖

Mitchell and Kobluk were relatively apolitical when the Chad Mitchell Trio began. Soon, however, they became activists. By 1965, they were guest celebrities at the Stars for Freedom rally in Montgomery at the end of the Selma march.

"We had come out of the Eisenhower period, which was very secure and safe and you did whatever you did by the numbers and you were promised a wonderful life," Mitchell says. "Why the kids changed, I have no idea, but they revolted against that. In a great number of cases, they were thinking that it was all a lie."

The late 1950s were "a very apathetic period for college students," says Kobluk, "and we were examples. We had no opinions, and there were few who did. Martin Luther King and the civil rights movement were making a lot of noise nationally, and college students started to take some of those issues as their own."

"For me personally, the civil rights situation was the first thing that alerted me," Mitchell says. "It also got to a lot of young people who were thinking for the longest time — especially if you weren't from the South — that everything's OK. It's been OK, and our parents are saying it's OK. But it didn't take very long for the college students to jump on that [issue] and say things aren't all right, and haven't been all right, and we're going to become aware of what's going on.

"Our material was ripe for their digestion at that point," Mitchell says. "There was almost nothing we could do on stage with our satire that they didn't get."

The trio were the first to record Bob Dylan's iconic "Blowin' in the Wind" when Dylan himself was a relative unknown, but their label refused to release it as a single because of the song's fleeting reference to death. Okun gave it instead to Peter, Paul & Mary, and it became one of their biggest hits.

Indeed, the trio dealt with censorship throughout their career. Kobluk recalled incidents during live interviews in radio stations where DJs would say, with a big smile, "Let's play a song!" Time and again, they'd pull out an album jacket with big black marks penned through songs that the station manager or the network had deemed too controversial for America's tender ears. In some cases, that meant most of the tracks on the album. "In a lot of ways, the material that we did helped us with the college crowd in live performances," Kobluk says, "but hurt us to the extent that we couldn't get the airplay that Peter, Paul and Mary did, or the Kingston Trio, or the Brothers Four, who did material that was not controversial and without a point of view."

The lineup of the Chad Mitchell Trio evolved over time and spawned some notable names, not the least of which was John Denver, aka Henry John Deutschendorf Jr. (seriously), who replaced Mitchell in 1965 when he left to do his own thing. Frazier befriended Denver, took him to his first peace rally and helped to shape his social views. The trio also launched the career of guitarist Jim McGuinn, who later changed his name to Roger McGuinn, formed the Byrds, and secured a spot in the Rock 'n' Roll Hall of Fame. When Kobluk eventually left the group in 1968, he was replaced by Michael Johnson, who later released his chart-topping "Bluer Than Blue" and numerous country hits after that.

Since his time with the trio, Mitchell has recorded three solo albums, sung for a cabaret in New York, worked in theater, attempted to start a vineyard in Oregon, worked as the director of entertainment for the Delta Queen Steamboat in New Orleans and worked as a realtor in Spokane, where he still lives. Now 70, Mitchell is retired but says he still can't keep up with his "things to do" list.

After a decade in show business, Kobluk moved back to Spokane from New York and finished his degree at Gonzaga — he had been a semester short when fame struck. A few years later, when the World's Fair started to materialize, "I literally camped out at King Cole's door," he says, and it paid off. Kobluk became one of the first dozen employees of Expo '74.

As Expo's Director of Performing and Visual Arts, Kobluk was charged with filling the brand-new Opera House during its premiere run in 1974. In October of that year, he was hired by the city of Spokane to run the Opera House — along with other facilities over his 28-year career with the city. Kobluk retired in 2001.

❖ ❖ ❖

Despite their decidedly political bent, the group never lost their sense of humor nor forgot that they were primarily entertainers. They're promising their fans a revised version of "The John Birch Society," rewritten by Congressman Dave Obey of Wisconsin to address more current affairs. Kobluk quotes Frazier as occasionally introducing a song today by saying, "The names have changed, but the issues remain the same." ∎

A tourist inside the United States Pavilion at the Spokane World's Fair.
EASTERN WASHINGTON STATE HISTORICAL SOCIETY PHOTO

Expo '74: 25 Years After

BY SHERI BOGGS

First published in the *Inlander* on April 28, 1999

This we believe: That the universe is a grand design in which man and nature are one.

That planet earth, a small part of the universe, is the residence of mortal man whose needs and aspirations are limited by the finite resources of planet earth and man's own finite existence.

That man is the custodian of his environment, as the environment is the custodian of man.

That man, in his growing wisdom, will renounce the age-old boast of conquering nature lest nature conquer man.

That the skies and the seas and the bountiful earth from which man draws his sustenance are the preserves of all mankind, and that in the brotherhood they derive from nature, the nations of the earth will join together in the preservation of the fragile heritage of our planet.

We believe in the restoration of the reverence of nature, which once filled our own land where the American Indian roamed in respectful concert with his environment.

We believe that the human spirit itself must set its own limitations to achieve a beauty and order and diversity that will fill the hearts of the children of the world with a new and happier vision of their destiny.

We believe that from this city of Spokane there goes forth to the world the message that the time of great environmental awakening is at hand.

All this, we believe.

— THE EXPO CREDO

On May 4, 1974, a world's fair opened in Spokane, the smallest city ever to host one. It became the living embodiment of a not-so-small miracle. For people who were either too young to remember Expo '74, or those new to the area, it's hard to imagine just how amazing and significant opening day must have been.

In the definitive book on the subject of Expo, *The Fair and the Falls*, EWU history professor William Youngs describes in great detail how Spokane was forever changed for the better by hosting a world's fair.

Just a year earlier, the fairgrounds were a squalid mess of railroad tracks, transient camps and industrial blight. Youngs says that "not only was there an industrial laundry on Canada Island that just belched suds straight into the river, there were plans at one time to actually fill in and pave the north channel of the river to create a parking lot." And former Mayor Jack Geraghty, who was in charge of public relations during much of Expo '74, says the Spokane River itself was particularly unimpressive, if not downright scary. "The river was nothing before Expo," he says. "Nobody would get anywhere near it but the 'knights of the road,' which is what we called the hoboes. It was just filthy."

But where ugliness and neglect once reigned, the first world's fair ever to embrace the environment as its theme had transformed the area almost overnight into a glorious fairground of lush grass and bright flowerbeds, all presided over by enormous metal and canvas butterfly sculptures that swayed gently in the wind. The pavilions set up all over the Expo site represented such nations as China, the Soviet Union, Australia and Iran, as well as commercial interests such as Kodak, Bell Systems, General Motors and Northwest Orient. The schedule of entertainers slated to play in the newly built Opera House in the coming months was like reading a *Who's Who* of early-1970s entertainment, with everybody from the Carpenters to Liberace to Up With People! set to entertain Spokane and her millions of visitors.

Opening morning, as 50,000 helium balloons and a thousand pigeons were being readied for their respective flights, President Richard Nixon was landing at Fairchild Air Force Base in Air Force One. Still, for those who were part of the nerve-wracking preparations — people like King Cole, president of the fair and chief proponent, Neal Fosseen, who had been mayor of Spokane in the '60s and a member of Spokane Unlimited, Petr Spurney, who served as Expo's general manager, and Glen Yake, chief engineer on the many demolition and construction projects engendered by

Expo — it wasn't time to relax and enjoy the day: not yet.

Geraghty recalls the mood among those who had worked so hard to make the fair a reality. "Right up until opening day, you don't even know whether it's really going to happen," he says. "There were so many things that had us worried. We were in the middle of a nationwide energy crisis, and the weather had been awful for weeks on end, but all of a sudden it's an absolutely beautiful day, and suddenly there are 85,000 people coming through this thing."

Despite jokes among the national press that the world's fair in Spokane would be, in the words of Youngs, "little more than a glorified county fair run by small-town hucksters," and in spite of concerns about a counter-fair being held by the Yippies (counter-culture activists with the Youth International Party) in People's Park, and even with a distracted, Watergate-weary President Nixon greeting Washington Governor Dan Evans at the airport as "Governor Evidence," opening day was, for the thousands of people who attended, incredible.

"It was magical, absolutely magical," says Youngs. "The natural setting by the falls was one of the finest of any world's fair. The sense of fun and goodwill was palpable. And there was a genuine sense of making a statement for good environmental practices — standing for something."

❖ ❖ ❖

The story of Expo '74 is essentially a story of urban renewal. By the 1960s, Spokane was well past her heyday, and businesses were leaving the downtown area in droves. To recent California transplant Cole, Spokane was a city in trouble. "All the time I'm thinking, what in the world is to be done here?" he recalls in *The Fair and the Falls*. "They had, it looked to me, like a pretty big problem."

Cole, who was hired by Spokane Unlimited, a coalition of local business and property owners, set about looking for a solution. First, he formed Associations for a Better Community, which brought together business and civic leaders interested in revitalizing Spokane from the inside out. Next, he started examining communities across the nation that had successfully turned themselves around. A 1965 visit to St. Louis, then in the early stages of building the Gateway Arch (located, ironically, where railroad trestles and industrial buildings once stood), proved significant. Cole returned to Spokane excited about the prospect of building a gorgeous park right in the middle of downtown.

To make such dreams a reality, Cole and other ABC members had to find a way to convince the railroad to relocate, and to generate the kind of funding such a project would inevitably require. With Spokane's centennial coming up, it seemed like some kind of huge celebration might be enough reason for the right purse strings to be gladly loosened. But by 1970, talk of a local centennial had shifted to the idea of an international world's fair, and by then, even some of the stubbornest opponents to progress were convinced. "There was a saying in 1974 that everyone who opposed the fair had left town," says Youngs, adding that in his research for the book, "I found almost no lingering opposition to the fair; but I encountered some complaints that the city government held the fair despite the opposition of the voters. But in actual fact, the voters favored a bond for the fair by a landslide. It was not enough to pass the bond, but it was enough to give fair backers a green light on gaining other means of funding."

And while it looked like Expo might be the trump card in the hands of those who would change downtown, the world's fair would ask in return a whole new level of commitment from the citizens of Spokane. Maurice Hickey, who ran the Bell Systems Pavilion for Expo, says that the best thing the world's fair did for Spokane was to bring about a shift in attitude. "It built a can-do spirit in this town," says Hickey, "not only within the business community, but the entire city got involved. We got the railroads to cooperate and get off the property, and it was like everybody was working together for a change. It was really a remarkable thing to see."

And once Expo was here, Spokane experienced an unprecedented level of activity. For those who worked in the exhibits, pavilions and restaurants, it was showtime every day for six months. "It was very challenging," Hickey recalls. "It was the kind of thing that very few people have done before. You had to make it up as you went along."

The Bell Systems Pavilion used a crowd management technique that Hickey laughingly refers to as "fill-and-spill." The auditorium had a multimedia presentation that ran every 20 minutes using 15 slide projectors and five screens. Hickey laughs: "It was top-of-the-line technology for the time." After the presentation, visitors were released into the exhibit area, where brand-new telephones dangled from the ceiling and a new emergency system, known by its simple code numbers 911, was being demonstrated. Over at the GM Pavilion, a similarly significant revolution was being displayed — the airbag.

By the time the world's fair closed in October, Expo had become a part of Spokane life. "Closing day was something of an anticlimax," says Hickey. "It was something we'd learned to live with and people got used to the activity. There was a certain amount of nostalgia, but we all knew, when it was over it was over."

Cole recalls that he didn't share in the tears he saw on closing day — after all, 10 years later, his mission was complete. "Somebody asked me, 'Why are you smiling,' and I said, 'Because it's over!' I didn't go back to the grounds for three years. In fact, I'd drive a different way to miss it."

❖ ❖ ❖

Like an enormous white sail against a clear blue sky, the U.S. Pavilion was both the visual focus of the world's fair and a reminder of the ideals that would shape the future of Spokane. Shaped like a huge, asymmetrical teepee, the U.S. Pavilion was a nod to the rich Native American heritage and local tribal traditions previously uncelebrated in the Inland Northwest. In predominately white, middle-class Spokane, Expo '74's emphasis on celebrating the diversity of world and indigenous cultures certainly represented a revolution in attitudes.

Bob Glatzer came from New York to coordinate a folklife festival at the fair for the Smithsonian Institution. When funding fell through from the Smithsonian, the Expo corporation took over the festival anyway and kept Glatzer at the helm. The festival, which ran for the duration of Expo, was a popular attraction. "We invited ethnic and cultural groups from all over the region to share their lives and culture with Expo visitors," says Glatzer, adding that, "there were games, crafts, cooking, music demonstrations, language lessons, all sorts of things, really."

Glatzer and his army of fieldworkers combed the region looking for pockets of Old World culture existing within miles of contemporary America. "We had about 30 groups in all," recalls Glatzer, "including a group of Basques from Boise, the Doukhobors, and a group of Russian Old Believers from Oregon." Glatzer goes on to explain the unique charm of Expo's Folklife Festival. "We were an odd appendage to the world's fair. Nobody in the Expo corporation had any idea what we did or why we were there. All they knew was that we were a great draw. It changed every day, sometimes every hour. We had logging contests every day, and gold panning where every now and then someone would find a real gold nugget. We even had a group of boat builders building a boat by hand for six months, and it was finished by the time Expo closed."

In addition to the folk cultures of the region, Expo brought thousands of people from all over the world into what was previously a strictly meat-and-potatoes kind of town. Food lovers who lived here prior to 1974 will recall that Spokane was by no means known for its restaurants. Geraghty emphasizes that "Spokane was never particularly a good restaurant city, but now it is." Glatzer concurs: "One of the really great things Expo did for Spokane was to bring more ethnic restaurants to town. I'm not kidding, there was nothing here in that way prior to Expo, and I think that the diversity that we experienced during Expo has a lot to do with our ability to support all the great ethnic restaurants that have sprung up since then."

For downtown merchants, Expo created a kind of boomtown ambience with people streaming in and out of shops from early in the morning to well into the night. North of the park, the newly renovated Flour Mill, with its railings and interior walls painted the wild day-glo colors of purple, lime green and orange, offered shops and eateries, including Clinkerdagger, with its incredible view of the river. South of the park, the downtown core was packed with visitors and new businesses (including a new Nordstrom store, its first outside Seattle). There was no such thing as an empty storefront.

But perhaps the most promising thing about Expo '74 was the story of the river. Youngs says the world's fair is "essentially a story of how we forgot the river, the reclaiming of the river and then the recovery of the river. It's absolutely astonishing how arresting it is to have a river running through downtown. Lots of cities have rivers, of course, but they're usually flat where ours has these incredible falls and it just runs rip-roaring right through the middle of downtown."

Cole agrees, saying they couldn't very well have an environmental theme without doing what they could to clean up the river first. "That was one of the biggest collateral benefits; years back, that river used to be an open sewer, you know. But leading up to Expo, the city rerouted its storm sewers and we got just about everybody to quit dumping into the river.'

Youngs paints an amusing picture of just how spectacular it was to build a world's fair around a natural feature like the Spokane River. "When Seattle hosted a world's fair in the '60s, they built the Seattle Center, which isn't exactly in the middle of Seattle nor was it on the ocean or anything — you could be in Iowa for all you knew. But here the river flowed right through the middle. The funny thing was how many visitors came up to the fair officials wanting to know, 'How did you get the river to come right through like that.'"

❖ ❖ ❖

Expo '74 laid the groundwork for many of Spokane's most celebrated institutions. "Expo introduced Spokane to different cultures, a new aesthetic, a new way of life," says Geraghty. "Hoopfest, Bloomsday, the Centennial Trail — all those things can trace their way back to Expo."

But while Expo seems to have been the single most transformative event in Spokane's history, there remains a nagging sense that we can still do better. As Hickey says: "Expo was really good for Spokane, but you can't hang your hat on that forever. We have to remember that was 25 years ago, and it's time to do something else."

Although Riverfront Park is one of the fair's most recognizable, beautiful legacies, the one-time U.S. Pavilion in its center has not been so lucky. Geraghty recalls that "there was talk of turning it into a headquarters for the National Park Service, which would have been perfect with Spokane being fairly central to all the great national parks in the West. But the federal government didn't have the money, so it didn't happen. It's unfortunate that we haven't transformed it into anything more meaningful than what it is now."

Youngs agrees: "This was the core exhibit, the cathedral, really, of the environmental world's fair. And now, for heaven's sake, the main pavilion area looks like a temporary amusement park in a grocery parking lot in a small town." Youngs adds that while he doesn't necessarily want to disparage the amusement park, he does "understand the dilemma faced by the Parks and Recreation Department, that unless the voters come up with the money, we can't build anything. But I think if we were to come up with a really great idea, more voters would be willing to get behind it." The Park Board is currently considering options for major changes to Riverfront Park, including options for a future use for the U.S. Pavilion site.

Beyond the uncertain fate of the pavilion, there is the larger issue of the city's relationship to the environment to consider. "We're not any more environmentally concerned than any other city," Glatzer claims. "For instance, the city just built a six-foot storm drain that opens out into the river just a few blocks from my house. And nothing was said about it; they just go and do these things and nobody says anything about it."

Youngs, who stridently opposes the building of any new bridges over the falls, points out that the area "is sacred ground, our great natural legacy, the most beautiful river setting in the middle of any American city."

"More bridges?" he questions. "That's like building a superhighway through Yosemite."

The subject of multiculturalism also brings up dubious response. "Every time I want to feel that Spokane has made great gains in terms of our multicultural awareness," says Glatzer, "then we come up against things like cross-burnings on church grounds and hate mail sent to black students at Gonzaga. I can't get very excited about any gains in this area."

Still, the world's fair has left behind an undeniable legacy at the very core of Riverfront Park and successive institutions like Bloomsday. Expo's lasting legacy is of a community that, once properly inspired, can come together to make amazing things happen.

Former Mayor and Expo exec Geraghty perhaps says it best: "It's interesting in talking about Expo, especially with people who are too young to remember it, that there's this notion that the world's fair is ancient history to a lot of people, which I suppose it is," he adds with a chuckle. "But at no other time in Spokane's history, with maybe the exception of the period right after the Great Fire around the turn of the century, have we all come together with such energy and vision to make something wonderful happen." ■

Mt. St. Helens begins to erupt on May 18, 1980; note the
Cessna's wing in the upper right corner of the photograph.

Flight With Destiny: Mt. St. Helens

BY TED S. McGREGOR JR.

First published in the *Inlander* on May 11, 2000

O ut for an early Sunday morning flight around Mt. St. Helens, Dorothy and Keith Stoffel wanted to see for themselves what all the excitement was about. As Spokane-based geologists, they were a little jealous of their West Side colleagues, who were closer to the action in the spring of 1980, when Mt. St. Helens started showing signs of a possible eruption.

The couple had heard of stubborn old Harry Truman, the proprietor of the St. Helens Lodge on Spirit Lake who refused to evacuate his home. On their fourth and final pass that morning, their hired pilot Bruce Judson took them right over the lodge and Spirit Lake, its still waters reflecting the blue skies and green trees that blanketed its banks. A red pickup truck rumbled down a road leading away from the lodge. Dorothy Stoffel noticed it was 8:30, and thought how peaceful it all seemed — how incongruous the scene appeared when matched with her geologist's understanding of what a volcanic eruption could mean for the landscape below.

At that moment, however, Stoffel had no idea how much her understanding of volcanoes would change. That's because the day of their flight was May 18, and as they gazed upon Spirit Lake, they were only two minutes away from an appointment with destiny.

As the small Cessna 182 crossed the north end of the crater that had been forming just below the 9,677-foot peak, the Stoffels noticed that there seemed to be more steam than they had seen on their previous passes. Suddenly they noticed the northern lip of the crater start to shake violently only 500 feet below their plane (caused by a 5.1 earthquake that was hitting just then). Soon a three-quarter-mile long cracked appeared, and a huge chunk of earth started to fall away (a landslide that turned out to be three-quarters of a cubic mile of earth — the largest ever recorded). Dorothy immediately became very scared, while her husband became excited over seeing what they had only read about in books.

As the plane continued moving east across the front of the mountain, it dawned on Dorothy that she could be witnessing the eruption of Mt. St. Helens. She realized there was no sound at all and mumbled "It's happening" to herself. Keith began yelling wildly about what he was seeing below. It took Judson to snap his passengers to action: "Take pictures, for God's sake!" he said.

Keith caught the landslide on film, and then captured the spectacular beginning of a powerful eruption of a gray plume of steam vertically and a black wall of rock, ice and ash horizontally. As he snapped his last shot on the roll of film, it became obvious that the giant cloud, shooting out superheated, steaming pieces of rock as it advanced, was coming right at them. Knowing the speed of a volcanic eruption (600 miles per hour) and quickly comparing that to the known speed of a Cessna 182 (150 or so), Keith and Dorothy began to fear for their lives. Dorothy could only think of what would happen to Larch, their dog, who they had left in the car at the Yakima Airport. Keith asked Judson: "Will we make it?"

"I don't know…"

❖ ❖ ❖

At 8:32 am, May 18, 1980, Mt. St. Helens erupted, and everyone — from the most experienced geologist to the most skeptical local logger — was stunned by the power unleashed that morning. In the hours following the eruption, Mt. St. Helens went from a 9,677-foot peak to an 8,364-footer. Those 1,300 feet went into the sky as ash and down the hillside as mudflows. It completely destroyed 156 square miles in a fan going northeast from the blast. It knocked down trees 18 miles away. The blast cloud was 30 miles in diameter and 63,000 feet tall; Mt. St. Helens ash was deposited as far away as Oklahoma. The explosion could be heard 1,400 miles away. (The Stoffels didn't hear anything because they were so close to the blast that the sound actually started outside of where they were located.)

And Mt. St. Helens took its toll on life, as well. The fear the Stoffels felt in those moments after the blast was mimicked throughout the region, which was filled by those who wouldn't follow the government's warning to leave, and by journalists and scientists trying to tell the story of Mt. St. Helens.

In all, 57 people died in the blast, including old Harry Truman, who survived being torpedoed on a troop ship in World War I and years on the lam as a bootlegger in California during Prohibition. Reid Blackburn, a 27-year-old photographer with the Vancouver *Columbian* was overcome and asphyxiated. And perhaps most famously, U.S. Geological Survey scientist David Johnston, 30, was killed moments after sending the famous radio message, "Vancouver. Vancouver. This is it." Johnston, his truck and trailer were literally blown off the ridge five miles northwest of the mountain. Today, Johnston is memorialized in the Johnston Ridge Visitor Center, the focus of the 110,000-acre National Volcanic Monument, which is located right on the site of the ill-fated USGS station.

The Stoffels and Judson, however, were not counted among the dead, even though they were by far the closest witnesses to the blast. As they flew away, Keith told Judson to head south, as the plume was moving north. Judson took the small plane into a nosedive to gain speed; he redlined the engine and achieved a speed of 200 miles per hour. As they looked back at the eruption, they saw a massive lightning storm with bolts tens of thousands of feet high (caused by all the charged matter entering the atmosphere at once). The bolts inside the ash cloud illuminated the crater, leaving the couple with a final image that has been burned into their memory ever since.

They knew they couldn't land in Yakima, so they flew to Portland. After they landed, Dorothy called their friends in Yakima and asked them to go retrieve Larch — and prepare for the coming ash cloud.

To this day, Dorothy and Keith Stoffel, who still live on Spokane's South Hill, thank Judson for his skillful escape.

"What he did for us has never been lost on me," says Dorothy today. "I've had 20 more years of life experience, including two children."

But even Judson's nerves caught up with him, as Dorothy recalls his comment just after landing the plane: "When you said 'Let's land in Portland,' " Dorothy recalls him saying, " 'I wanted to just keep going to San Francisco.' "

❖ ❖ ❖

The eruption's fallout didn't stop in the blast zone's radius. Throughout the region, people had to deal with the blanket of ash and massive mudflows. Melted ice and vast amounts of earth combined to clog the Cowlitz and Toutle rivers with mud and debris. Dozens of homes were destroyed, and so much silt built up that the U.S. Army Corps of Engineers had to dredge the Columbia River at its confluence with the Toutle and Cowlitz to allow barge traffic to continue.

Throughout Eastern Washington, including Spokane and Coeur d'Alene, the biggest impact was ash: tons and tons of ash. The closer to the mountain you were, the bigger the chunks were; in Yakima, the streets were covered with small pebbles, some the size of golf balls. But in Spokane, it was as if a dusting of fine, gray snow settled in over the city at about 1 pm. The ash was so thick coming down that the street lights came on in the afternoon.

At first it was just as exciting as a first snow of the year, with kids out playing in it and families taking tours of the city to best remember the occasion. But at City Hall, the mood was more serious, as they looked at it as a potential municipal disaster. No one knew what the dust would do to the sewer system, people's cars or even their lungs. As a precaution, school's were closed for a week, and most businesses closed for the first couple days after the eruption.

Terry Novak, who was Spokane's city manager at the time, recalls an organization that sprang to action, much the same way that happened during Ice Storm in 1997. Glen Yake, then chief of engineering services, became the city's point man during the crisis, which Novak says was managed with a minimum of hysteria.

By Monday, people were being told to stay indoors and not breathe in the ash. There was no evidence that it would be harmful, but public officials wanted to be careful. Then they managed to corral the entire Western United States' supply of particulate masks (like construction workers use when working with drywall), which they gave out for free so people could move around. Cars had a hard time as their air filters clogged up quickly, but the Spokane Transit Authority kept operating without interruption. Concerns about runs on supermarket supplies never materialized, and Spokane's sewer system never failed (as Yakima's did).

By Wednesday, kids out of school were spraying off neighbors' driveways, and people were collecting ash in jars for posterity (something you can still find at local garage sales).

As media attention from throughout the nation focused on Eastern Washington, Spokane Mayor Ron Bair, a TV news anchor prior to winning public office, became a familiar face on the evening news. President Jimmy Carter visited Spokane, but even he couldn't remove the thin layer of dust from across the region — fallout that continued to play a role in dangerous dust storms that kicked up along highways as long as 10 years after the eruption.

Nor could Carter dispel the national notion that Eastern Washington was buried and would perhaps never recover. Novak recalls making a trip to New York City not long after the eruption as part of a municipal bond issue and hearing firsthand how people back East thought Spokane was on its way to becoming a ghost town.

"The national media overplayed this thing to the point where they thought nothing green would ever grow in Eastern Washington again," Novak recalls. "They were saying we were going to be like the Sahara Desert out here."

Aerial photos proving that Spokane was, indeed, rising out of the ash convinced the bond dealers that Spokane would survive. At least until the next time one of Washington state's volcanoes decided to go off. ∎

Harold Balazs inside one of his creations in the yard of his Mead studio.

Veteran Eclectic: Harold Balazs

BY ANDREW STRICKMAN

First published in the *Inlander* on May 31, 1995

Our species creates myths when we discover that our most cherished truths are lies. One such myth is that of the artist as the uncompromising, rugged individualist overcoming all obstacles and ignoring everyday concerns to pursue a vision. There are mythic artists, of course, but I prefer the role of the anonymous craftsman, with an occasional body of work created in the hope of gaining immortality.
    — Harold Balazs, from an article in **Craft Arts International,** *1994*

And so are stated Harold Balazs' goals: To live a simple life, to do what makes him happy and to be remembered after he is gone. But don't count the 66-year-old artist out of the game yet; he certainly hasn't. Balazs (say Buh-lays) is an anomaly in these times of fiscal conservatism and lack of appreciation for the arts. For nearly 50 years, he's been married to the same woman, raised three children, traveled abroad and spent his life devoted to creating art. And he's actually made a living at it.

"The whole time it has been hand-to-mouth. It was better than that for about four years, but we're back to hand-to-mouth again. I suppose that's the way it's supposed to be," says the gray-haired man in blue jeans, eyes sparkling while he works on enameling an intricate lattice design in a lasagna pan.

A lasagna pan? Harold Balazs, the guy whose larger-than-life abstract sculptures sit in the Spokane River and on the water's shore by the Opera House? Harold Balazs, the artist whose design advice for medical devices including the Bagby Basket have helped people heal? Harold Balazs, the man who often calls young artists and asks them to come to his studio to impart some of their wisdom upon the old master?

Yes, there's a method to his madness. Lasagna pans, small lead figurines, garden sculpture and decorative mirrors have given way to large commissions, architectural projects and international notoriety as an enamelist. It also explains why he's been able to support a family.

"I'm a veteran eclectic," Balazs says from his studio, where he is preparing work for the 10th annual ArtFest — the only festival-type event where he exhibits. "I know for a fact that these art fair things have people coming through them with five or 10 dollars. My figuring is, there are people who would never spend $10,000 who would come to one of these things. My feeling is if they're going to spend five dollars, I might as well get it rather than the next guy.

"The idea that it's beneath your dignity or something like that is ridiculous."

❖ ❖ ❖

The meaningful moments of our lives are nothing but seeds, and it is only in memory they find a place to grow.

— Marcel Proust, on a paper scrap hanging in Balazs' studio

Driving through the woods, down the winding gravel road to the Mead homestead Balazs shares with his wife, Rosemary, it seems that anyone could be as prolific as this artist if only they could live in such a setting. Or, maybe, not get any work done at all.

The natural beauty that exists around Balazs' studio, 300 steps from his front door — a rushing creek bubbling beside an expansive garden, larger than life-size sculptures poking out of every corner of the yard and rays of sunshine flooding the yard through the old growth rising on all sides — is enough to make you unabashedly describe it as heaven on Earth.

"We almost lost it some years back," Balazs says wistfully as we climb the stairs to the second floor of his barnlike studio

"The biggest advantage of an environment like this is the house and the shop together. I maintain it's probably one of the reasons I've been able to survive.

"You get an idea late at night and you want to work on it, not commute for half an hour. The downside is that you become somewhat of a workaholic."

Balazs adds that living in your own slice of heaven does take some work. "We try not to be hermits, support the community. All of our children are here, and we've always been on deck to pick up grandchildren and such."

Every square inch of wall space throughout the artist's large studio is layered with art exhibit announcements, magazine clippings and scraps of paper holding words of wisdom from sages as incongruous as Proust and Bambi's mother. ("Thy blood-stained hands shall fry in Hell.") He is a voracious reader, consuming literature, then regurgitating it seamlessly within conversation.

Balazs' art has been called many things over his 45-year career: "revolutionary," "insightful" and "distinct" stand beside descriptions like "sophomoric," "crap" and, in some cases, "not even approaching art." But the criticisms are taken in stride, while the compliments are humbly accepted.

Born in Westlake, Ohio, and educated in art at Washington State University, Balazs first began approaching the business of art while still in school. Running a sign-making business with his peers gave him insight into the world of art-by-commission, and creating enameled jewelry with new wife Rosemary, then selling it through a gallery in Portland and at Spokane's Joel gift store, helped him learn about the concessions an artist must make to do what he loves and make a living at the same time.

"Many artists have worked in areas they don't want to work in order to put food on the table," says Beth Sellars, former curator of art for the Cheney Cowles Museum. "Harold is an example of perseverance in a community that doesn't support the arts, and has been successful in supporting himself and his family through his artwork."

A longtime skiing addiction found recent graduate Balazs on the slopes alongside architects who befriended the young artist and commissioned him to do large-scale pieces for homes they were designing. Front doors, fountains and functional sculpture all entered Balazs' frame of reference for what "art" is.

"I learned from my father's sheet metal business, a lot of techniques in metal and wood, so that I could sort of fake it when an architect asked me to make a door or whatever," he remembers. "I'm also very process-oriented. Just the process itself begins to dictate a way of working that opens up different doors. In that context, I think of myself only as an arranger of visual elements."

❖ ❖ ❖

Comparatively few people care anything about art, and when they do it's because they've mistaken it for something else.

— *A quote found by Harold Balazs' daughter*

Balazs' choice not to define the term "art" by other people's preconceptions has given him longevity in an otherwise cutthroat business, where fame is the only guarantee of a living wage.

"That whole star system we've created that focuses all the attention on the people at the top bothers me," he says. "People sit around and have arguments: 'Is Pavarotti, Domingo or Carreras the best tenor?' Of course, they ignore a whole raft of tenors who are probably equally as good because they've practiced more and not spent as much time trying to catch the spotlight."

And the avenue for artists to show their art has become more difficult to navigate as well. Galleries take much larger percentages than when Balazs first started — the most prestigious earning more than the artist who creates the piece.

"It used to be you had a show, you gave them a body of work and they hung it up. Now it's more of: 'Well I'll take this one, I don't like this one, that one might work.' It's no longer your show. It's the curator's show," he laments.

"More and more, Tom Wolfe's words from *The Painted Word* are reality. He said that the artists are no longer pursuing their vision, but are now trying to make their work conform to the notions of the critics and curators and people who run the art magazines and that sort of thing."

Balazs has occasionally tried to conform to preconceived notions of what art should be — emotional reactions and such — and usually with disastrous results.

"I was trying to deal with anger at one point and did a whole series of very sinister panels that were black on black — kind of Darth Vadery looking things. When I got them hung up, they just looked sort of designer chic," he chuckles. "It didn't work for me."

Instead of basing his work in reality, Balazs tends to take the tools of his trade — lids of washing machines, concrete, recycled aluminum, old farm implements — and uses them not in their intended form, but in some protracted, often humorous way.

Balazs laughs as he explains one of his pieces that pokes fun at reality. Hanging in one corner of his shop is a piece of farm equipment strapped to a board with the words, "Operate safely" printed above, and "See instruction manual" lettered below. A chain hangs off the bottom corner. Attached to the other end are the remnants of what was supposed to once be the "manual" but has since been ripped from the chain.

"A woman working where this piece was exhibited came up to me one day and told me that a bunch of people had reported the instruction manual missing," Balazs chuckles.

❖ ❖ ❖

He's a fountain of interesting discussion, and it's always well-grounded in literature. I usually listen to him with my mouth agape because he's just such a Renaissance man.
— Artist Ken Spiering on his mentor and friend

"Harold's work is a kite of glorious colors tethered to reality by a very thin thread," says friend and local artist Ken Spiering, known for his giant Radio Flyer wagon in Riverfront Park, and as the designer of the annual Bloomsday poster.

"He first approached me in '83 by coming to my show and purchasing a painting. He'd been doing this with other artists. He just felt some sort of drive to reach out to young artists, and we became very close.

"Without exception, Harold contacts me, calls once a week, checks to see if I'm still alive," continues Spiering. "He's become a dear, dear friend and mentor. He's a standard in my life that I try to live up to but never will — the pure industry of making artwork, the effort it takes."

Spokane Art School Director Maureen Davidson gives a similar assessment: "I think he's an incredible role model for all of us, artists or not, in how to live our life — in being intelligent and thoughtful."

Davidson's and Spiering's comments give additional perspective to the impression of Balazs as a man for all seasons. He often has visiting artists come to his studio where they exchange techniques and stories, frequently trading art pieces in the process. The inside of the Balazs home is artistic in and of itself. But the works that populate the shelves, hang from the high ceiling in the living room and adorn the walls are testament to his devotion to the discipline that brings him joy and pays the bills.

"I often find myself being on the receiving end [of criticism]. There's a lot of people who believe I conspire to keep other local artists from getting commissions around here. That couldn't be farther from the truth.

"How do you enter the art market these days? For young people, it's so much harder than when I got started," he admits. "Every year I go over to talk to Patty Haag's class at the Falls and it gets harder every year. It's just a lousy, lousy time for single proprietorships."

Yet Balazs is continually searching out the talented in Spokane's creative ranks — whether they're a visual artist, musician, actor or strong mind of a different sort — offering whatever encouragement he can.

"I would like to see something happen once a year where you have a venue for all-comers — anyone who wants to present [their take on art]. There's something about that cross-pollination that works and brings people out of the woodwork.

"There's a lot of very shy people out there and they happen to go to a curator, a gallery owner somewhere, who isn't particularly interested in that idiom, so they turn the person down or reject them. I think people in those positions need to be more catholic than they are. I've seen so many cases of where 'quality' just too often means, 'the idiom I prefer.'

"More and more I think the creative mind is needed everywhere," Balazs continues. "In our education system, as soon as anyone demonstrates what could be considered a 'creative mind,' we shove them into the arts — assuming that's where creativity should go."

❖ ❖ ❖

Although my ego has been wounded occasionally, I am reminded that truth is the first sacrifice when seeking acceptance into exclusive groups.
— Harold Balazs, **Craft Arts International** *article*

Balazs, while paying slight attention to criticism of his work, is not afraid to wield the scepter himself. Of particular frustration to him is the conflict between making art and making a living.

"I told the students the other day, 'If you're planning on going through galleries, expect 70 percent of it to go to other people.' That's kind of a hard reality to accept. A lot of young people are now looking for alternate ways of doing it."

An artist who has never directly received a National Endowment for the Arts grant, Balazs still stands up for the idea of publicly funded art — after all, many of his larger commissions have been created with funding from city and state governments.

"A nation that professes what we profess and then to have something happen like what's happening now with arts funding is just unconscionable." he says. "If I had to make the cut to the NEA — and I wrote letters suggesting this — cut the funding to individual artists and maintain the funding for the institutional organizations.

"Manufacturing napalm is justified because it creates jobs. But when it comes to art, that doesn't count. Everyone thinks these things are just created out of vapor.

"They don't want to admit the realities. That piece of mine that floats in the river was a $33,000 commission. My out-of-pocket on that was $27,000. I bought $10,000 worth of stainless steel; doesn't that count for creating jobs for miners, distributors, warehousemen and all that? It's such a short-sighted, crazy issue."

Balazs, while a staunch advocate of artistic freedom, doesn't find value in shock art — that which oftentimes obscures its quality by trying to express an artist's emotions.

"I went down to see Kiki Smith [an NEA-funded artist, making a presentation at the Cheney Cowles Museum]. To me it was about the most sophomoric thing I've ever seen." he explains. "She dealt with body excretions and those parts of the body that ooze things. One of the sculptures was a nude woman on her hands and knees with a 40-foot turd hanging out of her.

"I don't see that as ennobling the human condition in any way. The fascinating thing about the evening was her philosophical justification for doing this, but I found it of very little redeeming social value."

He admits that while there are plenty of artists who can stretch our imaginations without offending, getting in the public's face also has its benefits. "But when you're in a time like this and you've really got the Jesse Helmses after you, maybe rather than getting in someone's face, you tread a different path," he begrudgingly admits.

Balazs' work has never worked on a shock level — it tends to be more conjured, abstract and eclectic than that of his contemporaries. His sense of humor pokes holes in all things pompous and bombastic, but inevitably has elements of reality sewn throughout.

"I've always felt our notion of dignity is usually a mask worn by people without it. So most of my work tends to be kind of whimsical except for the stuff that came out of Australia. I was so intrigued by that country's makeup."

A trip to Australia last year gave Balazs the fodder for a glass-on-metal series based on Aboriginal pictographs.

"I've also always been fascinated with pictographs, and the marks people have left from generations past, and I've been fascinated with the importance ascribed to them," he says. "Nobody has considered the fact that maybe this was just someone trying to jerk the future around."

Balazs and Spiering have done just that in recent years, creating thousands of small clay pieces with childlike sketches etched into them.

"When we go on canoe trips and such, we leave some of these scattered about. I would just love to know what people think they've found," he says with a laugh. Occasionally, he gets to find out.

"A month ago, St. John's had been graffitied," Balazs says. "I had just finished putting up some doors for the Unitarian Church — the building is almost Shaker-like, but the doors are very gestural, just black on white. These people were approaching the building and their child said 'Oh my God, mom, they got our building, too.' It was one of the best compliments I'd ever received."

❖ ❖ ❖

Tell me and I will forget. Show me and I may not remember. Involve me and I will understand.

— writing on a wall at Balazs' studio, author unknown

Very little has caused Harold Balazs to ever slow down. When he fractured four discs installing his Japanese-style, 15-foot tall sculpture in front of the Opera House a number of years back, he spent his eight-month convalescence painting a series of watercolors.

"I try always to look at what I can now do, instead of, 'Oh, look what I've had to give up,'" he says of the experience.

The same goes for his life in general. When a knee replacement finally caused the artist to give up skiing ("It was the most important thing to me outside of family and work"), he took up sailing and helped design a boat that he now sails on Lake Coeur d'Alene.

He and wife Rosemary go whitewater canoeing, and he loves spending time with his grandchildren. "It's so fun to watch the children, to rediscover things like running around with a bug net. Most people my age, they're nice and everything, but they just seem so dead."

And that's one place Harold Balazs doesn't expect to be — ever. "As Woody Allen says, 'I'm not afraid of death, I just don't want to be there when it happens.'"

But Balazs doesn't have to worry about being *there* when it happens. His art and life's work will have guaranteed him spots in many places — just like the immortality be continues to search for. ■

The restored Martin Woldson Theater at the Fox,
with the resident Spokane Symphony on stage.

Marquee Names: Fox and Woldson

BY TED S. McGREGOR JR.

First published in the *Inlander* on November 15, 2007

H e filed the lawsuit that busted Thomas Edison's monopoly over the movie business. He introduced the system for movie sound that is still used today. He was the first to film in widescreen format. His name is on one of the world's biggest TV networks, on a movie and television studio and even on a certain downtown Spokane theater that starts its second run this week as the newly renovated home of the Spokane Symphony Orchestra.

Meet William Fox, the most famous American you've never heard of.

It's a rags-to-riches-to-rags story any of his screenwriters would have loved to write: Hungarian Jew immigrates to the United States, penniless; entrepreneur parlays a single Brooklyn theater into one of the largest entertainment empires in Hollywood; mogul sees it all slip away as the Great Depression descends.

"First and foremost, he was an entrepreneur who was totally, totally oblivious to risk," says Susan Fox Rosellini, William Fox's great-granddaughter. "As he built his business, the whole thing was always on the table, and his innovations helped create the media as we know it today. The sadness I have is that the world has not picked up on that and sung his praises."

❖ ❖ ❖

To right that historical wrong, Susan Fox Rosellini and her husband Donald spent 10 years researching and writing *William Fox: A Story of Early Hollywood, 1915-1930*. Rosellini points to an all-or-nothing gambit to purchase the MGM movie studio and theater chain as the turning point in 1927. Fox's bid was built on short-term debt and doomed by bad timing; in 1929, the stock market crashed. In fact, by the time the Fox opened in Spokane in 1931, William Fox was no longer the owner; mounting debts and federal anti-trust investigations forced him out in 1930. Ultimately, a smaller competitor was able to swallow Fox's empire, and thus was born 20th Century-Fox Studios. Far from penniless but out of the Hollywood game for good, Fox retired to New York and died in 1952, forgotten by the town he helped build.

Amid all the setbacks, Fox's studio cranked out hits; in the very first Academy Awards of 1929, Fox won five Oscars for *Sunrise*. In 1930, Fox Pictures' *The Big Trail*, starring John Wayne, was the first-ever movie filmed in widescreen.

The movie business was changing quickly in the 1920s, and Spokane can be thankful for that.

"All of the moguls went into integration," says Rosellini from her home in Key Biscayne, Florida. "If they made the movie and they owned the theater, they had somewhere to show the movie. The theory was to vertically integrate."

So Fox, Paramount, Loews and others started building their own theaters; Fox owned about 1,000 theaters, about 300 of which he built. Theaters became more and more elaborate, as architects competed to make a trip to the movies an escape to a different world. An ad that ran just before the San Francicso Fox opened in 1929 read: "Here in this Fox dream castle… is the utopian symphony of the beautiful, attuned to the cultural and practical… No king, no queen had ever such luxury, such varied array of singing, dancing, talking magic, such complete fulfillment of joy."

"Remember, this was a world where there's no TV, not a ton of radios in homes yet," says Rosellini. "In those days, this was the entertainment — the theater itself and the movie."

Rosellini adds that in her research, she found that it was her great-grandmother, Eva Fox, who oversaw the interior decorating of the theaters her husband was building during his spree.

As nice as it is to see her great-grandfather's name on Rupert Murdoch's properties, Susan Rosellini is just as proud of the theaters he built —

especially the 25 or so that have been saved. She still recalls bitterly the demise of the San Francisco Fox in 1963, and her grandmother was involved when saving the Fox in Atlanta became a major political saga in the 1970s.

"The tragedy of those theaters is that so many of the beautiful ones got knocked down," she says.

So this week, somewhere, William Fox is smiling — but he might be turning over just a bit in his grave, too. Due to the purchase agreement the Spokane Symphony signed with the Fox's previous owners, Regal Cinemas, no movies can be shown there until 2020. Oh well, as Fox would have known, that's just business.

❖ ❖ ❖

Now, just as we're getting to know the man the Fox Theater was named for back in 1931, there's a new name associated with Spokane's grand old theater. With a $3 million gift, the Martin Woldson estate helped start the process to save the theater, and now his legacy will forever be associated with the project, as the new name is, officially, the Martin Woldson Theater at the Fox.

Woldson and Fox would have been kindred spirits: Like Fox, Woldson immigrated to America; before he was 20, Woldson was working for James Hill's Great Northern Railroad. Woldson settled in Spokane shortly after the Great Fire of 1889 and became one of the West's best-known railroad problem-solvers. He even had the audacity to create the Lewiston Grade, one of the craziest stretches of road anywhere.

Woldson passed away at the age of 94 in 1958, not long after Fox, but the fruits of his labor live on through his daughter, Myrtle, who made the gift, citing her father's love of music and the performing arts. ∎

Walt Worthy in 2001, with renovations and reconstruction of the Davenport underway.

INLANDER PHOTO / AMY SINISTERRA

Saving the Davenport Hotel

BY WILLIAM STIMSON

First published by the *Inlander* on September 13, 2012

One day in June of 1985, as Tim Babcock turned the key to lock up the Davenport Hotel one last time, he felt it — the end of a glorious era. He had tried, but nobody wanted to buy the faded ghost of what had once been among America's greatest hotels.

Babcock, a former governor of Montana and a partner in the latest effort to save the Davenport, had a theory on what caused its demise. Every owner who followed founder Louis Davenport, he told the *Spokesman-Review*, put the minimum investment into the hotel and hoped to grow rich on its past glories. The hotel was allowed to become obsolete and frayed. Now, said Babcock, the hotel required a really big investment — tens of millions of dollars. Someone was going to have to — as the poker term says — go all-in.

"Somebody's really got to want to do it for it to work," Babcock said. "The hotel simply has no other way to go."

Babcock had been showing potential buyers through the hotel in hopes of finding that big-time investor. They all uttered "wow" at the lobby and the big rooms, then their enthusiasm wilted as they surveyed the vast needs of a 60-year-old, 14-story structure that covered a city block.

One of the people Babcock showed through the hotel was a 39-year-old local contractor by the name of Walt Worthy, who was unlikely to be able to afford the hotel. In fact, Worthy thought it was extremely generous of Babcock even to take the time to show him around. Worthy had a good look at why so many buyers said no thanks. The floors upstairs were warrens of too-small rooms and broken plumbing. Then Babcock took Worthy to the basement.

"It was totally scary, looking at all those pipes," Worthy recalls today, "miles and miles of pipes going to who knows where."

Nevertheless, Worthy made the best offer he could muster. As he expected, it was rejected.

There were no offers acceptable to the mortgage holder of the bankrupt hotel, and so that June day, Babcock had no choice but to pull the doors shut and turn the key.

❖ ❖ ❖

After two decades of warnings, the closing of the hotel should not have come as a surprise to Spokane. But it did. The Davenport Hotel was not just another business. Nearly everyone who had been in the region for any time had pleasant memories connected to it: graduation dances, weddings, honeymoons, Christmas dinners, anniversaries. The hotel, a sampler of the glittering palaces of Europe, was something grand Spokane had to itself, right here in the middle of the great savanna of the Inland Northwest.

People started calling each other: *Did you hear about the Davenport?* City councilwoman Sheri Barnard organized one of her big meetings. Kathryn Gellhorn, a South Hill institution already known for her work raising money for the arts, started dialing numbers from her fat book of contacts. She alerted Edna Mae Brown, who lived in a mansion on Sumner Avenue with her husband, Thoburn, a retired industrialist; the Browns had their wedding reception at the Davenport Hotel in 1940. Then she called Norma Stejer, wife of Richard Stejer, probably Spokane's best-known banker after 50 years at Washington Trust Bank.

Out of these calls grew the Friends of the Davenport, an organization with a board of about a dozen people and a membership that would eventually grow to more than 2,000 dues-paying members. The story of the Friends of the Davenport is really the story of a lot of stubborn women (and most of the group's leaders were women) protecting the Davenport like it was their child.

The Friends wanted to "keep the lights on" by opening the hotel periodically for public events so people wouldn't forget what they had.

Their other purpose was to "keep the heat on" — that is, to remind the owners of the hotel, who were in Texas, that a decision to tear it down was not going to be taken lightly by Spokanites.

The group did what they could to capture the interest of possible investors. Board member Nancy Compau, archivist for the Spokane Public Library, did research on the hotel, which two architects on the board, Marian Evanson and Dave Shockley, organized into an informational kit. Other board members drew up lists of hotel chains and investors who might be interested. Norma Stejer personally delivered sales materials to the New York City office of hotel magnate Donald Trump.

The mantra was, "Try Everything."

The Friends arranged with the owners of the hotel to open the doors for Mother's Day in 1986. They were amazed when 2,000 people showed up. Every Christmas, the Friends decorated a giant tree in the lobby and opened the doors for a "Davenport Christmas." Hundreds of people paid a $10 donation just to see the building again.

Still, it often felt like a futile effort. The few prospective buyers the Friends rustled up would come by to look at the building. Without exception, they shook their heads and departed. And some in Spokane actually wanted it torn down, arguing that a dark, empty building cast a pall over downtown.

Ellen Robey, who served as president of the Friends of the Davenport for 13 years, recalls: "People would stop me on the street and sort of pat me on the head and say, 'Oh, Ellen, why don't you put your energy someplace else. It's just a beat up old building.'"

Then suddenly, in 1990, the hotel had a buyer — an international hotel chain, in fact. The unlikely connection came about because a man by the name of Jim Hill had started his career in hotels in Spokane and then had gone on to work for several major chains. Now he was working for Sun International, based in Hong Kong. Hill convinced his boss, Wai Choi Ng, that the hotel in Spokane was underpriced. If it were purchased, Sun could fix it up for resale or find an American partner to share the cost of reopening the Davenport.

The Ng family bought the hotel and did the first significant rehabilitation to it in 30 years. They cleaned it up in general so it would show well. They refinished the oak-paneled Elizabethan Room to give a better idea of what the whole hotel could be. They also cleaned the World War II-era tar off the lobby's skylights, so that the space had the daylight glow that had been intended when it was built.

❖ ❖ ❖

Just when things seemed to brighten for the hotel, it assumed a new burden. Spokane's local electrical utility, the Washington Water Power Company, announced in 1994 that its old steam plant a block south and uphill from the Davenport had been spilling oil underground for decades — an estimated 75,000 gallons of it.

At the very least, the oil spill was one more liability that would have to be explained to already skittish buyers. Sun President Wai Choi Ng announced if the oil was not cleaned up, his company would not be able to sell the Davenport and would have to close it again.

The Friends of the Davenport conducted its own study and in March of 1996 released an eight-page report that was mailed to its list of approximately 2,000 members. The report began: "Spokane is in danger of sacrificing the Davenport Hotel in order to preserve an oil spill." It urged members to write letters to Washington Water Power and to newspapers.

The board of the Friends was packed with people with long resumes of service in civic and arts circles. Just one of the signers of the Friends report, for example, was board member Dorothy Powers, who, after 40 years as a reporter, columnist and editorial writer for the *Spokesman-Review*, was a name as familiar and as respected to Spokanites as the Washington Water Power Company. Powers was a fierce defender of the hotel: She met her husband Elwood at the Davenport, and spent her wedding night there, too.

As the annual stockholders' meeting of Washington Water Power approached, the Friends decided someone should go and register their complaint about the oil spill. Several members had WWP stock and so could speak. Norma Stejer stepped forward. "I got to looking, and I realized I had more stock than some of their board members."

Stejer, a tall and striking woman, ignored the three-minute limit allotted for comments and lambasted the group with phrases like "should be ashamed" and "lacking civic irresponsibility."

"All I remember," Stejer said later, "was the president of Water Power kept saying, 'Thank you, Mrs. Stejer!' and 'We understand, Mrs. Stejer!' But I just rattled on." At the end she drew an explosion of applause.

Not long afterwards, the chief lobbyist for WWP scheduled a meeting with the Friends board and asked them what they wanted WWP to do.

Soon trucks were on First Avenue drilling holes and pumping out spilled oil, the Ngs shook hands with WWP executives and the hotel was being shown to potential buyers again, including one Walt Worthy.

❖ ❖ ❖

"It had such great bones," Worthy says today. "It's one of the most incredible buildings in the nation."

Karen Worthy, Walt's wife and business partner, recalls all the times he'd drive past and stop his car, just for a moment, to look at it. "He used to sit across the street in the parking lot over there," Karen says, pointing through the hotel's Palm Court Grill window across First Avenue. "He'd say, 'I would sure like to buy that. I think I will someday.' I'd say, 'Sure.'"

Walt Worthy, a native of Georgia, arrived in Spokane in 1968 as a young airman transferred to Fairchild Air Force Base. He was assigned to teach survival skills to flight crews headed for Vietnam. This involved being in the field for long stretches; when he returned, he often had many days off. Since he was making around $80 a month in the Air Force, Worthy searched for profitable ways to use his spare time.

He began salvaging cars in auto wrecking yards and fixing them up for resale. He rebuilt and sold a couple dozen. One day he fell into a conversation with a contractor who was desperately looking for a subcontractor to do some roofing work. Worthy didn't know anything about roofing, but he knew a guy who did. Worthy signed that guy up — and two others — bought some hammers, "and the next morning I was in the roofing business."

That night, he discovered he had already lost $100 on the deal.

Now he looks upon such reverses as a kind of tuition. "There's a learning curve to everything you do," Worthy says. The trick, he adds, is to learn faster than you lose money.

"When you make mistakes and you have to pay for them, you learn a lot faster than when you're working for somebody else," he says. "That's the thing a lot of people skip in my mind, is getting the opportunity to make their own mistakes and having to pay for them."

It's a philosophy shared across many decades with Louis Davenport himself, who, when he was first starting out in Spokane in 1895, told the *Spokesman-Review* that: "I am learning something every day, and expect to as long as I am in the business."

Worthy kept learning, too, but soon enough stopped paying tuition. He saw a "For Sale" sign on a lot on Spokane's South Hill, so he decided to build a house on it and sell it. Again, he didn't have the slightest idea how to build a house. "I didn't even know that studs were spaced on 16 inches."

But another man was building a house up the street. "I'd go over and watch what he did and go back and do it on my house." Worthy finished the house and sold it at a good profit. Then he bought another lot.

By the time he was mustered out of the Air Force in 1972, he already had some experience in building. He went looking for building opportunities and soon, with the help of small crews of three or four, owned several apartments and other buildings.

One night he and Karen were at dinner with a friend who happened to mention the state was looking for office space to lease. Walt had a building that was empty and submitted a bid "at a very reasonable price." They got the contract and went looking for more buildings to recast into office space. Later he built the successful Rock Pointe Corporate Center on a tricky outcropping of basalt near the Spokane Arena. Eventually, Walt and Karen Worthy became the largest provider of state office space in Eastern Washington.

❖ ❖ ❖

Meanwhile Jeffrey Ng, Wai Choi's brother, was sent by Sun International to manage the hotel and try to sell it. But he had fallen in love with the Davenport, too. Walt kept in touch with Ng and told him, "If everything else fails, I'll be your buyer of last resort."

One day in 2000, Spokane was hit by a freak windstorm and a gust picked up a large sheet of tarpaper from the roof of the Davenport and dropped it on Sprague Avenue. This caused the city to close the street with barricades. Worthy happened along and offered to send his team to help secure the roof. This gesture led to a telephone call from the Ngs the following Monday, and consequently resulted in the sale of the hotel the following Friday.

Because the hotel was a business that had been failing for 40 years, had been closed for 17, and the fact that Walt and Karen Worthy had no previous hotel experience, the banks were reluctant to loan them any money for the purchase.

"I wouldn't have lent me any money either," Walt says.

So the Worthys sold off most of their other buildings, except Rock Pointe, to raise the $40 million needed to purchase and restore the Davenport Hotel.

They were all in.

No one knew what would happen when the doors opened — for the second time — on Sept. 13, 2002. "It was better than I ever dreamed," Walt says.

Then it just got better and better. Now, on the 10th anniversary of the reopening, Worthy reports, "This last month was the best month we ever experienced."

"One thing we didn't count on was the people," Worthy continues, "how badly they wanted the Davenport to open."

He gives a lot of the credit for the success of the Davenport Hotel to its many promoters in Spokane.

"People ask them, 'Where should we stay?' And they say, 'The Davenport.'" ■

Inside the Kennel during the 2012-13 Gonzaga basketball season.

INLANDER PHOTO / YOUNG KWAK

Zag Nation

BY MIKE BOOKEY

First published in the *Inlander* on March 7, 2013

A steady snowfall has turned to freezing rain on the campus of Gonzaga University. It's cold and getting colder, and everything is taking on a thickening layer of ice, including the tops of some 80 tents tightly packed into what would be a grassy knoll, were it not the middle of a January in Spokane.

For the past two days, this has been the home to a rotating cast of about 400 students. The previous night, it was so cold university security sent the kids inside. Some of them protested the move. They actually *wanted* to camp in what would turn out to be a 15-degree night. It's all part of the deal.

A freshman from northern California emerges from a tent, a friend immediately zipping the flap behind her. She makes it a few steps between tents, but the ice wins and she's immediately on her back. Letting out a sigh, she doesn't move, staring up at the sky as if to remind herself, again, that this is all part of the deal.

This is Gonzaga basketball — if you want to be close to the court, this is what you have to do. In 36 hours, she'll be in the first few rows of the 1,250-strong student section, screaming her head off on national television as Kelly Olynyk doesn't miss a shot in a 20-point drubbing of Brigham Young University inside the McCarthey Athletic Center.

"Yeah, that happens a lot," says James Lumia, wincing as his fellow fan picks herself off the ice and gingerly makes her way through the maze of iced-over nylon.

Lumia, a junior political science major, is the camping and tickets director for the Kennel Club — the school's student cheering section that's gained almost mythical status in college basketball during its 29 seasons — and he's presiding over this seemingly ill-advised camping trip. He's quick to point out that these kids aren't willfully sleeping in tents in order to get tickets to the game. No, they got those four days earlier. This is just to get close to the court.

"For the most part, if you don't love basketball when you come here, you're going to learn to love it," says Lumia.

❖ ❖ ❖

A month and 12 consecutive wins later, an Associated Press poll ranked the Gonzaga men's basketball team No. 1 in the nation this week, ahead of Indiana, Duke and Kansas. It was yet another breakthrough for a program that has spent the past 14 seasons doing little else: winning an unprecedented number of conference titles; a nearly unrivaled string of NCAA tournament appearances; a streak of 20-plus-win seasons that has reached 16; producing three NBA first-round draft picks. All the while being led by Mark Few, a coach who some believe has reinvented the way we think about how a college basketball program is built.

Almost impossibly, a small school in Spokane has become one of the best programs in college basketball, with the national following to prove it. This is a team that has changed a university and a city and instilled a culture that is the envy of other programs. You can't isolate one specific source for this phenomenon. There were certain shots that went in, certain players who signed a letter of intent to play here, coaches who decided to stay put, fans who'd travel to the ends of the earth, and perhaps most important, a city like Spokane that could help all these pieces fall into place.

It almost makes sleeping in sub-freezing elements understandable. Almost. But then again, some of these students came here precisely to do this.

"We came to a game in fourth grade and saw the student section and knew that was going to be something we wanted to do," says freshman Kate Sessler, bundled up inside a laptop-screen-illuminated tent with her twin sister, Maddie. The two grew up in Tacoma, and this is cold for them, even if they're using the mattresses from their dorms to keep off the frozen ground.

It's not like everyone who arrives at Gonzaga is there expressly for basketball. In fact, it appears the Sessler sisters are in the minority when it comes to this. But there is something called the "Flutie Effect." This is the often hard-to-verify phenomenon of an increase in a school's enrollment and number of applicants because of the success of its athletic program. It's named after the increase in applications at Boston College in 1985, the year after eventual Heisman Trophy winner Doug Flutie tossed a legendary Hail Mary to knock off Miami on national television.

At Gonzaga, this reality of this phenomenon is hard to argue.

In 1999, the year the ongoing run of NCAA tournament appearances began, undergraduate enrollment at Gonzaga was only 2,747, making it one of the smallest schools in that year's NCAA tournament. Undergraduate enrollment for the current academic year is 4,906. The student body has grown by 79 percent in a mere 13 years. During that same period, acceptance rates for incoming freshmen dropped from 88.5 percent to 66.6 percent. In 2011, the rate was as low as 61.6 percent.

With the increased enrollment came a slew of improvements to the university, spearheaded by the vision of then-university president Fr. Robert Spitzer. In 2003 alone, the university improved its housing, added 30,000 square feet to its business school, 37,000 square feet of science space, and announced plans for new student housing. The following year, the shrine to the basketball program, the 6,000-seat, $23 million McCarthey Athletic Center, opened in time for the 2004-05 season. More new facilities and campus improvements continue to build on what was, even a decade ago, a small and slightly stale stretch of Spokane.

At the same time, the Gonzaga Nation, if you want to call it that, had spread far from the Spokane city limits or even the Pacific Northwest. Television deals were reached, apparel made it far and wide, and players became household names across the country.

❖ ❖ ❖

The story of Gonzaga basketball, as it's often told, goes something like this: No one had really heard of Gonzaga until they made a run through the NCAA tournament in 1999. Wearing royal blue uniforms as the announcers consistently mispronounced their name, the tough-nosed squad coached by Dan Monson knocked off Minnesota, Stanford and Florida before losing to eventual champion Connecticut in the Elite Eight. Then, with Mark Few at the helm, the country had a chance to fall in love with the likes of Casey Calvary, Richie Frahm and a slew of others as the Zags (people realized you could call them that) went to two more consecutive Sweet Sixteens.

There was Dan Dickau, an All-American who played in the NBA. The team, now with a gregarious big man named Ronny Turiaf, continued to dominate the West Coast Conference, all the while appearing more frequently on ESPN and convincing major programs to play them during the non-conference portion of the season. Next, there was a new state-of-the-art arena just in time for the ascension of Adam Morrison, who had a mustache, read Karl Marx and could score 40 points even with his hair in his eyes. The Zags just kept winning and winning, with Jeremy Pargo and Elias Harris and now Kelly Olynyk. Eventually Spokane, and then a lot of people far from Spokane, came to love them dearly.

Explaining the Gonzaga phenomenon in this manner is like saying the Beatles became huge stars because people liked the melody of "I Want to Hold Your Hand." It's just scraping the surface.

For two men sitting in a bagel shop just a block off the Gonzaga campus, it all started long before that fabled run. Jack Stockton remembers when this building was an IGA grocery store back when he opened Jack and Dan's Tavern, just across the street, in 1961. He's sitting across from longtime friend Jerry McGinn, a former United Press International (UPI) reporter who wrote some of the first national sports stories about Gonzaga basketball.

But that's not how they know each other — they both grew up in the working-class Logan neighborhood that surrounds the constantly expanding campus. Much of their old neighborhood is now part of Gonzaga, but Stockton can still list the names of the families who lived in those now-gone houses.

They trade stories about seeing games at the tiny gym Gonzaga once called home — it's now been converted into the Russell Theater. It held just a couple hundred people, and McGinn would find a way to sneak into games. Stockton remembers a time when a fight broke out between Gonzaga students and fans traveling from Montana. They laugh, remembering an era of the university's basketball program that very few others can relate to.

Soon, conversation turns to Jack's son, John, the NBA Hall of Famer, who like his dad grew up right next to the school. This is where McGinn says the foundation of Gonzaga's dominance was built.

"Along comes this kid from the neighborhood, which is amazing, and turns out to be a Hall of Fame point guard and one of the best to play the game," says McGinn.

"*The* best," says Stockton.

It's McGinn's theory that it was here that Gonzaga basketball began creeping into the national college basketball consciousness.

"Every time John's dribbling the ball, and every time he went up and down the court, there would be a reference to Gonzaga. So now there's a reference to Gonzaga every week on TV. As he became the player he became, it became a continuing advertisement for Gonzaga," says McGinn.

Still, this didn't translate into sustained success. It might have laid a foundation for what was to come, but Spokane had yet to fully embrace their Zags.

Across the street, Bob Finn, the Gonzaga alumni director, is sipping a beer inside Jack and Dan's. The place is about half full, and Finn seems to know just about everyone, who, just like him, are wearing the requisite navy-and-red Gonzaga gear that's all but required this time of year at Jack and Dan's. While everything about the school and its basketball team has gotten bigger, sexier and slicker, the small-town feel of Jack and Dan's remains. While the students will likely flood in and the music volume will increase later that night, during the afternoon it's as much of a neighborhood hangout as you're likely to find in this city.

Finn transferred to Gonzaga from Eastern Washington University to play baseball in the mid-'80s and became the second president of the Kennel Club. It was not the organized swirl of a thousand highly devoted and organized kids in matching shirts that it is today. Then, it was Finn, his baseball teammates and a couple dozen others — totaling maybe 50 or so, all of them men — who'd meet up for beers before the game and then unleash a torrent of insults upon visiting players.

It was fun, he says, but the team was never amazing during his undergrad years.

"I'm not sure if we were ever much over .500," says Finn. He motions across the restaurant, and shouts — "Hey, Jeff! What was your record your senior year?"

Jeff Condill, a standout guard who graduated in 1986 and is now a co-owner of the bar, thinks for a bit.

"I think we were 17 and 15," he says.

He's close; they went 15-13 that year. Still, Finn says, it wasn't anything like it is now, and there was no sign that the program and the Kennel Club could become anything other than just something to occupy their time.

"There was no premeditation that this was going to be anything. We just thought it would be a fun thing to get us through the next few years of college," says Finn.

But looking back, Finn realizes there may have been a less tangible quality about the university that made possible the kind of run that began 10 years after he graduated.

"Did we think it was going to be a big thing? No, but everyone there had a similar feeling. They didn't know what it was about that school, but there was a community there that was hard to explain," says Finn.

The freezing masses huddled in their tents before the BYU game in January talked about that same sense of community. A priest came out at 11 pm and said Mass. Pizzas were delivered. Students emerged from the relative warmth of their tents to hang out en masse in the middle of the makeshift scene.

In all, there are about 2,200 registered members of the Kennel Club. That's about 45 percent of the undergraduate student body and almost a thousand more than the McCarthey Center student section, says club president Connor Cahill. He's put in the time to keep him from needing to camp out on a night like this, managing, along with a board of directors, a student-run group that is now officially part of the athletic department. It's a well-oiled machine, capable of ushering between 600 and 700 students down to the West Coast Conference tournament in Las Vegas.

"Alumni come back and think about their GU experience and it's the Kennel Club. It's jumping up and down to 'Zombie Nation' and what that means," says Cahill, a senior from Portland who already has a job lined up in the biochemistry field — meaning he has ample time to devote to this program in his final semester.

"Zombie Nation" refers to the techno song "Kerncraft 400" that has become a staple of the Gonzaga pre-game ritual. It's as impressive as anything you'll see in college basketball. A coordinated dance full of jumping, deafening stomping, and arms-over-one-another swaying, it's perhaps both intimidating and odd, and maybe corny, to an outsider.

But to students, it's an encapsulation of how this program has created a community within the student body, and vice versa.

Few has said that the student body's efforts give the Zags an eight-to-10-point advantage, and opposing players and coaches might be inclined to believe that. The power of the Kennel Club is something that has taken on an almost mythical reputation. But perhaps for good reason — the students travel well (including large contingents at games as far away as the brutal one-point loss to Butler in Indianapolis in January), can be deafening, and truly feel like they're part of this phenomenon. After they graduate, they come back as the sort of dedicated alumni who continue to bolster the school's athletic programs.

But the Kennel Club, or any other student section for that matter, doesn't win games. That's about as bluntly as Jay Bilas, a longtime ESPN basketball commentator who hosts the network's weekly *College GameDay* show, puts it.

"I know [the Kennel Club] has a lot of fun and they're really into it. Now I'm going to be unpopular saying this, but I don't think fans can influence wins like that. Also, I don't recall fans ever taking responsibility when we lost. I'm of the opinion that crowds are part of the atmosphere," says Bilas.

The wins, he says, happen down on the court.

❖　❖　❖

On the last Monday in February, after a pair of blowout wins against Santa Clara and San Diego, Few is standing, arms crossed over a long-sleeved Gonzaga T-shirt, looking out as his players shoot around before practice. Reporters are asking at the time how it feels to be the second-ranked team in the country, and he's giving boilerplate responses about how they've earned it and how it's nice to get the recognition. From the court, a shot goes awry and the ball rolls his way. Arms still crossed, still talking to the reporter, he gives the ball a kick. It lasers to the chest of senior forward Guy Landry Edi, who catches it.

"*Niiiiice*," Edi says with a smile at the coach who recruited him from a junior college in Texas.

Few doesn't smile. In the style fans have become familiar with over the past 14 seasons, he's stone-faced, always with an eye out on the court as he fields a few more questions about what it means to be ranked this high, and to have accomplished yet another first for a coach who has spent most of his career exceeding the expectations of those around him.

"He's one of the best coaches in the country. I'd put him up there with anybody," says Bilas.

Few, already a longtime assistant coach by the time he took over from Monson after the Zags' 1999 Elite Eight run, has won more than 70 percent of the time against an increasingly tough non-conference schedule. He's also a successor to the late coach (and athletic director) Dan Fitzgerald, who former players and coaches credit with helping to establish the culture that surrounds the program. If you talk with former and current Gonzaga players, they'll describe what sounds like a lifelong fraternity from which most players never seem to stray too far. This is one of those intangible elements that goes into Gonzaga's victory soup — players like the other guys around this team, in the same way that fans are attracted to the players.

Despite all the on-court success, the WCC dominance, the NCAA tournaments, the *Sports Illustrated* cover stories, Few says one of the things he loves most about what's happened at Gonzaga is the fact that so many of his players never drift too far from this program.

"It means everything to me. That's probably the neatest aspect of the job — having ex-players feel so good about their experience that they come back here to settle down and start their careers here, and basically spend their life here," says Few, taking his eyes off the court for the first time.

"That means everything to me. What that really says is how well they're treated in Spokane, and that says everything about this community," says Few.

On a recent Saturday afternoon, two of those former players who came back to Spokane are coaching their 7-year-old sons' basketball team. Dickau, the All-American point guard who played six seasons in the NBA, is sitting on the bench, giving the sort of high-fives and back slaps that were undoubtedly ingrained in him during his playing career. Out on the court is Jeff Brown, wearing a Gonzaga warm-up jacket and looking every bit of the 6-foot-9 he used to become the 1994 WCC Player of the Year, scoring 21 points per contest for a team that won 22 games. But on this particular afternoon, there are no fouls, no traveling and they don't keep score. Brown is out there pacing the court and reminding the kids they have to dribble.

Now the executive vice president of sales of Next IT, a Spokane-based information technology company with 160 employees, Brown has remained very much in the fold of the Gonzaga family, but he's still surprised sometimes by how much has changed since his playing days.

"Mark Few, at that time, was a grad assistant and making, I think, $1,500 a year and teaching tennis classes. My wife actually took a class from him," says Brown with a laugh. "The types of guys they're recruiting now are far more talented. But to also see that Kelly Olynyk was named a first-team academic All-American is special stuff."

Former Gonzaga players work for the university, they're lawyers, they run businesses, they call the radio and television broadcasts, and many find other ways to remain visible and influential in the Spokane community.

"[Former players] like being around the program, and they had a phenomenal experience living in Spokane," says Brown.

Olynyk, a Canadian 7-footer who took last year off to develop his game, has come to understand the university's relationship with its city.

"The community has really rallied around the program and the program has brought life to the community, so it's a mutual relationship that's really working in a place like this," he says.

This might all just sound like flowers-and-rainbows feel-good stuff — and maybe some of it is — but there's a more pragmatic side. Former players, many of them playing professionally or still maintaining a strong skill set, need a place to work out in the summer, and that benefits current players. In the early days of Gonzaga's NCAA run, John Stockton was still playing for the Utah Jazz and would go toe-to-toe with active players, shaping the game of many of the school's skilled point guards a decade ago. It's still happening these days.

"In the summer we'll have 10 guys playing here. You get experience against guys who are playing at the NBA level and get tips from them," says David Stockton, John's son and a fourth-generation Gonzaga student.

Few knows the impact these former players have made. The way he puts it, his intent is to create a team that's much larger than the names listed on the roster.

Bilas, a guy with firsthand experience with nearly every successful basketball team in the country, says the type of players and people who come out of this school has become one of the program's best selling points.

"The coach is the most important part of any program, but what sells Gonzaga better than anything is the players. When you visit there and get to know these guys, that's one of the biggest attractions," says Bilas.

❖ ❖ ❖

People want to know how this happened. Coaches and athletic directors around the country are wondering why they don't have students camping out before games, and why they haven't sold out every single game since their arena opened. They want to know why they can't forever shake the dreaded "mid-major" tag and make a run that spans two decades and places their team logo on the rear windows of half the cars in their city.

"There are other really good coaches out there, and really good programs, but to expect that other people can do this is like to say that everyone needs to be John Wooden," says Bilas over the phone from Milwaukee, where he's about to call a Marquette-Syracuse game. "It would be folly to say there's a secret sauce they're using to accomplish this."

Even for a former Zag like Brown, the basketball program's accomplishments and the growth of its fan base is still something that inspires awe.

"This became something that went from lightning in a bottle to the brand of Gonzaga being America's team, and walking through airports in Chicago and seeing a Gonzaga basketball hat. This has fundamentally changed. This was not a one-hit wonder," says Brown. "At the end of the day, now this is something that's unprecedented."

It may be unprecedented, but that doesn't mean everyone has accepted the fact that a team like Gonzaga could be the top-ranked squad in the country. Zagmania is not universal. In fact, you don't have to get too far away from Spokane (or *in* Spokane, if you've ever visited the *Spokesman*'s message boards) before the bubble breaks and dissenting voices pour in.

"FYI Gonzaga is Notre Dame Football 2012 — only difference is we have a tourney #noonethinkstheyarethetrue#1," tweeted CBS basketball commentator Doug Gottlieb the day after then-No. 1 Indiana was thumped by Minnesota, opening the door for the Zags to rise to No. 1. He's referring to how Notre Dame was ranked at the top of the BCS, only to be destroyed by Alabama in a championship game that revealed the Irish probably should never have been ranked that high.

Another CBS commentator, Seth Davis, went a step further, claiming that Gonzaga shouldn't even be a No. 1 seed, even if they are No. 1 in the polls going into the NCAA tournament.

Others, like *Grantland* writer Mark Titus, a former Ohio State benchwarmer and author of the ESPN offshoot's Top 12 NCAA Power Rankings, acknowledged the backlash that Gonzaga gets from its critics. Titus, who hilariously has referred to Gonzaga as "the Foreigners" all season in his column, wrote this in defense of Gonzaga: "You remember that friend growing up who would turn off video games at the last second when you were beating him so that he could say that you didn't actually win? That's what America is doing to Gonzaga right now. 'Nuh-uh. You can't be the best team in the country because, um, because it's just not fair!'"

A lot of college basketball fans are probably saying this, but they've got some ground to stand on. Gonzaga doesn't play in a major conference, and the conference they do play in handed them some serious blowouts this year. They don't always look as flashy as the teams ranked below them, and some think they get more national media attention than they deserve.

Those statements are mostly true. But those are also the factors that make Gonzaga what it has become — the No. 1 team in the country.

But given the sort of expectations that Gonzaga fans have built up over the years, there is still plenty to prove. Despite continued success, the Zags haven't made a deep run in March since that first magical year. They've never reached the next level of recognition that allows them to be mentioned alongside the Dukes and North Carolinas on a consistent level without starting an argument. No matter how beloved this program is adored by its students, its city and its fans, there's a sense that there's more out there.

A visibly exhausted Few acknowledges this as he sits courtside in Provo, Utah, after the Zags squeaked past BYU last Thursday night. It was a slugfest — sometimes quite literally — marked by poor shooting on the Zags' part and a high level of emotion amplified by BYU's sell-out, boo-at-everything crowd. And to raise the stakes, third-ranked Duke had just lost at Virginia, arguably leaving the No. 1 ranking for Gonzaga to grab with a win.

With the ESPN headset awkwardly draped over half his face and speaking with former-coach-turned-commentator Bruce Pearl via satellite, Few was asked what this season has meant to him.

"We've done a lot over the years at GU. The only things we haven't done are get to No. 1, get a one seed and win 30 games," Few says. "Maybe it's time we start crossing some of those things off the list." ■

ABOUT THE AUTHORS

TONY AND SUZANNE BAMONTE are historians in Spokane, publishing their work with the Tornado Creek publishing house. Past titles include *Spokane's Legendary Davenport Hotel* and *Miss Spokane*.

SHERI BOGGS was a staff writer and arts and culture editor for the *Inlander* from 1999-2005.

MIKE BOOKEY has been the *Inlander*'s culture editor since 2012.

ROBERT CARRIKER is the Alphonse and Geraldine Arnold Distinguished Professor of the College of Arts and Sciences at Gonzaga University, where he has taught for five decades. He is also the author of *Father Peter John DeSmet: Jesuit in the West*.

MIKE CORRIGAN was the first freelance writer ever hired by the *Inlander* in 1993; he was a staff writer from 2000-05.

NICHOLAS DESHAIS was an *Inlander* staff writer from 2008-12.

EMALEE GRUSS GILLIS is a Spokane-based writer.

PATRICK HEALD was a freelance writer for the *Inlander* from 1993-95.

LISA WAANANEN JONES was the *Inlander*'s web editor from 2012-14.

MICK LLOYD-OWEN was an *Inlander* staff writer from 2006-08.

TED S. McGREGOR JR. is the founder and publisher of the *Inlander*.

IVAN MUNK was a Spokane artist and historian who contributed to the *Inlander* from 1994-2000; Munk died in 2006.

RON MYERS turned his hobby of reviewing old local newspaper archives into the story "News of the Year: 1899."

JACK NISBET is a naturalist and historian in Spokane. His books include *Sources of the River*, *The Collector* and *Visible Bones*.

WILLIAM STIMSON is a journalism professor at Eastern Washington University and author of *A View of the Falls: An Illustrated History of Spokane*.

ANDREW STRICKMAN was employee No. 1 at the *Inlander*, serving as arts and culture editor from 1993-1996.

KEVIN TAYLOR was an *Inlander* staff writer from 2005-11.